A View Into the Mind of Asperger's
Book 3 - Boarding the Train

A View Into the Mind of Asperger's
Book 3 - Boarding the Train

S. Lea

I Street Press

© Copyright April 2021, S. Lea

All rights reserved. No portion of this book may be reproduced, stored in a retrieval system, or transmitted in any form by any means – electronic, mechanical, photocopying, recording or otherwise – without prior permission of the copyright owner.

Lea, S.
A View Into the Mind of Asperger's
Book 3 - Boarding the Train by S. Lea

ISBN: 978-163795664-9

Library of Congress Control Number: 2021901163

Cover Design by Web Imagine

Illustrations by Janet L. Rau
Editor – Janey Ranlett
Continuity and Proof by Janet EG
Technical Advisor - JAC

FIRST EDITION

Printed in the United States of America.

I Street Press
828 I Street
Sacramento, CA 95814

To the California State Railroad Museum

To the staff, the docents, and the crew of the Sac Southern...past and present.

Thank You for the profound influence you've had on our lives.

Preface

Third in the Train series, "Boarding the Train", is an attempt to provide something that I never had almost two decades ago, when my son was diagnosed with what was then called a Verbal Learning Disorder. Over the years this condition has become part of the Autistic Spectrum and is now more commonly called Asperger's.

    All those years ago there was very little information on the condition and even less on how to face its challenges. There were no suggestions for parents on how to improve the day to day life for these children, their siblings, or their extended family.

    Readers of "Chasing Trains" and "Waiting for Trains", the first and second books in this series, will notice some of the same material is covered here in "Boarding the Train". I could not assume familiarity with the first two books, so I felt it necessary to include certain, important information.

  This book focuses on activities and events related to my son going out into the world, more independent and away from the safety of home and early school. I knew he would no longer always be under a watchful eye, so I continued to use his overwhelming passion for trains as a tool to enhance his 'worldly knowledge', and hopefully help him to get through day to day encounters.

  Continuing to support my son was paramount, but that support now came more in the form of getting him where he needed to go, and less on my involvement with what he did once he got there.

  As my son matured, this series matures as well. The topics in "Chasing Trains" were more isolated, and specific, producing immediate results. In "Waiting for Trains" I partnered with the outside world and sought out ways to help him deal with the inevitable challenges he would face over time.

  This third book in the series becomes much more story telling. It describes activities and experiences that would shape him over time. It relates more of how we lived, and the things we did together, that resulted in positive outcomes.

  I still had to be very diligent, but by then I had the luxury of fuller communication with my son and together we could discern what actually was or wasn't working, in terms of moving forward.

    It is a serious subject, but I again try to put things in focus. Life is an adventure and can be entertaining at times. I want my target audience, other parents, to get something from this book and want to do it in a way that will be interesting to everyone.

Contents

Preface		i
Introduction		1
Chapter 1	The Lunch Bunch	7
Chapter 2	Curtain Call	15
Chapter 3	Road Trip	21
Chapter 4	Class of 45	33
Chapter 5	It's Always a Good Day at the Museum	43
Chapter 6	Dust Bunnies	53
Chapter 7	A Carefree Summer…"Indeed"	61
Chapter 8	The Girl from Ipanema	69
Chapter 9	Senior Ball	79
Chapter 10	Getting Past Q & A	85
Chapter 11	Harvest Moon	93
Chapter 12	Car Attendant	105
Chapter 13	Olympics	113
Chapter 14	"There's No Crying in Welding"	119
Chapter 15	Pulling Out of the Station	133
Acknowledgments		136

Introduction

Like the first two books in this series, "Boarding the Train" is also intended to share information with other parents of children diagnosed with Asperger's. Information that was not available to me all those years ago when a diagnosis of Asperger's was actually quite rare. Information that I hope will help make day to day challenges a little less taxing.

In the early years as my son and I struggled with communication, as I struggled to understand the source of his meltdowns, I continued to try different things, hoping to discover something that would help him. Once I found, sometimes quite by accident, a method that worked, any change I introduced seemed to have immediate effect.

A minor change in his attire, a change in the way I would say something, a change in our morning routine, often had positive results in our daily life. If I discovered anything that made our daily life more rewarding and less stressful, I grabbed it and ran with it. This is not indulgence. This is survival. This is a mother's instinct that anything that helped my son live daily life with less turmoil would do the same for me.

Although I continued to work on making our daily lives rewarding, he would be going out in the world now.
It would be important that I promote his success over the long run.

As he grew older the changes and adjustments were more of a process. As the boy matured, the process of change matured as well. There was much more planning, and much more thought, put into making decisions about daily life as well as activities in the bigger world.

In some ways this was easier…I could test something out over time and make adjustments later…In some ways this was more difficult, because if I "got it wrong" I would be back at the starting gate.

As he moved on from the protection and monitoring at middle school, he would now be in the high school world. Although there would continue to be support, no daily monitoring was afforded. He was becoming a young adult, and would have to depend more on his own skills.

Thankfully, I was in fairly close contact with the folks who supported him, but I still wanted to make sure he was in a safe environment and had an exit plan if needed.

During that time we made a trek out into the world, our road trip, along with his cousins. This was very influential in his life as it was less about me, and more about experiencing things "with the guys".

Then came what would be the most important part of his progression into early adulthood. He was recognized, not only for his passion for trains, but also for his expertise. Becoming a Docent and eventually Car Attendant at the Railroad Museum was a multi-faceted win.

We would still experience communication issues, but now at a higher level. I would have to "check my frustration at the door" when I had to balance his accomplishments with the fact I still wasn't always clear when he described his day.

As he grew more independent he was not always happy with my 'hovering', but we eventually moved on to a place where we could enjoy our mutual interests together.

He continued to be a very interesting fellow. He would often surprise me with his ability to see things, sometimes better than I saw them. The continued 'literal thinker' would often put me in my place, with no specific intention of doing so.

Like any other parent I had to recognize that as my child moved out into the world, I would have to balance protection with freedom. You have to hope and trust that what you have instilled in them will get them through.

    With an Asperger's kid there is an added fear, an added trepidation, because the world may not always see the behavior in the same way you do. It is important that they get along…but it is also important that, even as young adults, you still counsel them on what they need to be diligent about. You still must talk through possible scenarios, and how to read the signs around them in a proper way.

    The early books were much more about specific issues, specific events or routines. In this book you will have to indulge me as I write a bit more about experiences. I write more of a "story", a story that is meant to capture the things that influenced my son's life.

    I hope you will be entertained, and also be afforded ideas that might work for you and your child. I hope you can move through life making sure to picture your child independent someday.

    As always, my "suggestions" are just that. They are intended to communicate things that worked for my son and me. They may not work for you, but by processing the information you may come up with ideas of your own.

CHAPTER 1

The Lunch Bunch

Back in the "olden days" when I was going to school, the progression was elementary school, to junior high school and then on to high school at sophomore level. As ninth graders in junior high school, we thought we were "all that".

The first day of high school was definitely a humbling experience. We were no longer at the top of our game. We were no longer the 'upper-class'. We had been knocked off our pedestal and now had to face the reality of being the low guy on the totem pole, once again.

As schools mimic society, there seemed to be a 'pecking order'. In the first few weeks of high school it was up to us to discover that particular order of things.

For the bullies of junior high, they now might become bullied themselves. For the top performers on the basketball team, they now might face being the shortest guy on the team. For the academic standouts, they might become just mediocre talent.

During my son's years in school the progression was somewhat different. He went from elementary school to middle school, middle school being simply 7th and 8th grades. Then from middle school, he was on to high school as a freshman, at the ripe ol' age of fourteen. I was terrified.

He would not only have to face a new and unfamiliar environment, he would be expected to function more independently and be on his own, much of the day.

Unlike middle school, where I was contacted and offered an opportunity to meet with staff to discuss my son's details, my only job in high school was to simply drop him off on his first day, and hope for the best.

In the first few weeks of high school it was paramount to me that my son had a good experience, as it would likely set the tone for the next four years.

As parents we hope that our children attend class, have good teachers, and learn what they can. Just as importantly, we want them to have a good day and feel good about their surroundings and friends.

I had the luck of receiving a flyer in the mail regarding an orientation and a 'parent's night' scheduled a few weeks before the start of my son's freshman year. I jumped on that like a 'hot potato'.

I was pleasantly surprised when, once again, I discovered the school district had coordinated his transition. I found out on parent's night that in addition to having, like all students, a resident home room teacher, he would also have the support of a one, Mr. Lee.

Mr. Lee, a leader in what this school district called the Strategies Program at my son's high-school, was tasked with supplying that added connection and added support my son might need. He was also my son's math teacher.

As before, I anticipated that it might become frustrating and difficult to figure out what was going on at school when I talked to my son directly. He would likely give me 'piecemeal' facts, and I would have to seek out more information to put the puzzle together. Meeting Mr. Lee on parent's night gave me that 'go to guy' to fill in the blanks when they needed filling.

The first order of business was Mr. Lee explaining the "Lunch Bunch." This was a group he had put together for the first few weeks of school. They were required to report to his classroom at lunch time to eat and do some homework.

He of course was providing a safe and predictable environment for those in his charge, and an opportunity to more slowly adjust to this new life in high school. His "Lunch Bunch" consisted of many kids who had known each other since middle school but included many others who had come from other schools.

Over the course of the first semester these kids could continue to come to his classroom at lunch, but were no longer required to do so. As they felt more comfortable with their surroundings, they were as free as any other student to have their lunch in the quad or cafeteria.

As my son attended his classes, got the 'lay of the land' and met up with other students, he and his buddy would often start venturing out at lunch on their own.

I anticipated possible issues but made sure that my son was prepared. This was not yet a time to ask him "if this happens, what will you do.? It was not yet a time yet to ask him for feedback and then possibly have to correct him when he got the answer wrong.

Instead, I would talk to him about many possible scenarios in his day. With each scenario, I would offer a good suggestion on how he might deal with a challenge. It was not yet the time to have him face an issue unprepared, un-discussed and just hope for the best.

Unfortunately my concern for the social issues, and the bullying issues, were not my only concern. We were already dealing with guns at schools, gang-bangers, and just a general sense of unease that schools were no longer the safe havens they once were.

 I made sure my son understood that if he was with his buddy, or on his own, and was approached by unfamiliar students who gathered around him asking questions 'not quite right' he should leave the area and get to Mr. Lee.

 If he was approached by students who seemed to 'like him' and wanted to laugh a lot but he didn't know them, he should probably just get to his next class.

 If he met up with class buddies, knew them and was having a good time...it was OK to feel good about it.

 I told him in the classroom and at P.E. he would always be fine. If there were any issues, simply raise your hand and ask your teacher or your coach to clarify what you should do.

 Don't underestimate your child's ability to read a social cue, but don't assume your child will be totally aware of what's going on as they are still young and might be dealing with others much older. Unfortunately they might be faced with older kids who are cruel. Don't cry later...prepare them for the exit they may need to avoid a bad outcome.

 All in all, the first several weeks in high school were critical to what would come. If you don't have the good fortune of a school with good programs, than it is up to you to reach out to teachers and counselors that can help.

You can bitch and moan and groan, but ultimately, it's up to you to reach out and make sure your child is in a place that works, even when life is 'unpredictable'. If you reach out, you will likely find a teacher or a staff member or a counselor who is more than willing to help your child.

If there is no 'lunch bunch' in these first trying times of high school for your child then contact teachers, other parents, counselors, or anyone you can, and make sure there is an extra set of eyes watching out.

I have heard from parents that didn't prepare and simply "hoped for the best." In some cases it was OK, but unfortunately in other cases, it was only after the fact, after an incident, after the sorrow, that they were compelled to set up a plan for their child.

Suggestion

Don't wait until school has already started….have a plan in place for your child on the very first day.

Chapter 2

Curtain Call

In his freshman year my son took his core academic courses, reading, writing, science and arithmetic… One of his electives was a Children's Theater class.

He didn't chat much about his classes but on one occasion he told me he needed to bring some supplies to his Children's Theater class. Quite frankly, I don't remember the exact nature of the supplies but I do remember having to fill up a bag with the required contents.

When I was dropping him off that day, he had a very heavy back pack and some gym clothes so I offered to carry the bag to his Children's Theater classroom. This classroom was a bungalow adjacent to the school parking lot. Although his first period was homeroom, he said he could drop off the bag before his regular classes started.

    I walked with him to the classroom and entered with the bag. I was greeted by his teacher, who was a very jolly fellow. We shook hands, and to keep my son's potential embarrassment to a minimum, having his mother in tow, I left the bag and proceeded to leave.

    Without my asking, his teacher began talking about what a great student my son was. He indicated that, not only was my son pretty talented, he was also "a pretty funny guy".

    Given my son was more of an introvert and not a big "talker" this news was a bit surprising. On the home front he was a more serious sort and when I would make a joke he didn't seem to find it all that funny. Picturing him as a "pretty funny guy" in this classroom environment was a welcome surprise.

    Maybe at home it was just bad at jokes on my part? Maybe, when it comes to parents, nothing is funny? Either way, I was convinced that the Children's Theater class was having a positive influence on my son. Performing children's plays, with lots of funny characters and funny stories, gave him an opportunity to see the silly side of life.

    At some point I remembered back years and years when, during one of his assessments, a specialist did mention that getting my son involved in theater classes would be helpful. At the time I didn't give it much thought.

Given these kids sometimes lack the ability to read cues and the world around them makes no sense, with theater they know what to expect. In the world of theater things are predictable. Like all actors, they are prepared for what is going to happen, and even more important know how to respond.

With scripts to memorize they have no doubt about what they are expected to say. When they have a drama coach directing the interaction between characters, they can start understanding, and be comfortable with, the dynamics of communication between two people.

All these years later I understand value of theater. He was in an environment where he was clear on what he was expected to do. He was part of a group where he was finally on an equal playing field.

In that environment he thrived. In that environment parts of his personality were coming to the forefront as never before. He understood the proverbial 'joke' along with the rest of the group.

At home I still was 'not funny', but I was happy that over the next few years theater classes would always be part of his class schedule. They became core courses in his educational plan and that paid off.

Suggestion

Consider theater as part of your child's curriculum.

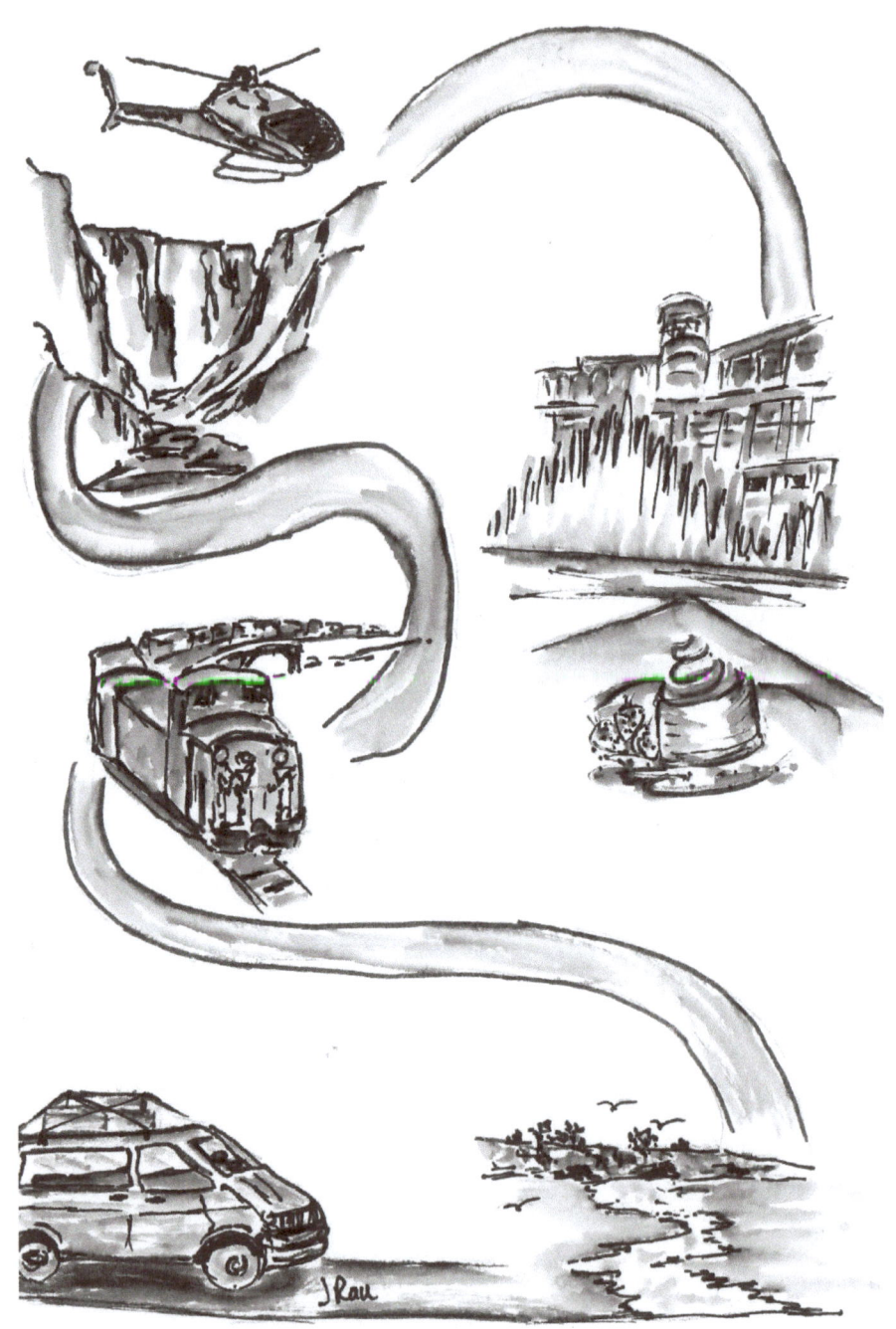

Chapter 3

Road Trip

Over the years one thing that remained constant was the benefit of a routine. Predictability kept things calm and enjoyable. Up at the same time every day, to school, and an evening meal as close to 6PM as I could manage, would always make for a less stressful day.

I knew that as important as our regular life was, I still needed to get my son out in the world to see 'bigger things'. This meant traveling, either by car or plane to expand his world.

I would always prepare him far in advance for the event or upcoming trip by wrapping it around something that included his passion. If I wanted him to see Yosemite Valley, what better way than to make the

Yosemite Mountain Sugar Pine Railroad part of the trip?

By promising a trip to a wonderful excursion train location I was able to get him excited and positive, even though it would take us out of the comfort zone of daily life. From a relatively early age, I was able to get my son "out and about", destination train trip, and successfully expose him to all sorts of really wonderful things on the way. I was again using his passion for trains to teach him about all the other things going on in the world.

We would travel to many places just to get onto a train for part of the day. But on the way we would visit towns and valleys, mountains and deserts, seashores and forests all along the way.

Over a few summers my nephews helped out by watching over their cousin while I was at work. They needed to make a 'few beans' and I needed to go to work every day knowing that my son was in a safe and happy environment.

One summer, as I looked at my nephews, I became painfully aware they were growing older and would be moving on to lives of their own. I knew this may be the last chance to engage them in a few short weeks of hanging out with their aunt and young cousin. They meant the world to me and I couldn't imagine how life was going to be without them there on a regular basis.

I pulled out all the stops. I called in every offer for credit cards I had received. I looked at renting a van but realized, for the price of two weeks, I could make six months of payments so I bought a van. I started planning a road trip and hoped my nephews would want to come along. After all, what better companions than people who do not just know one another but know each other well.

I presented my case to my nephews and to my son with a rough draft of my plan. I was ecstatic when not only did my nephews agree to this trip, my son agreed as well. He was excited to be traveling to destinations with his cousins, rather than just his Mom.

A trip to the AAA office for maps was completed. The phone calls and on-line reservations were made for our hotels along the way. Boarding arrangements for the pets were taken care of.

We would depart in a few weeks. Knowing that eating restaurant food for two weeks would take a toll, I prepared and froze meals to put in an ice chest for the trip. At least for the first few days we would be eating home cooked meals.

Besides the usual jeans and shirts, shorts and swim trunks, my mom and I took them all shopping to purchase slacks, and shirts and ties, for a surprise I had planned. This surprise would be at our final destination.

The day came, we all converged and with smiles and waves from my mom and sister, we headed out. The van packed to the point where the back two tires would likely need some extra air.

Fortunately we only got a few blocks before I realized I had forgotten to load the ice chests with the home cooked meals. We turned around, headed back, my mom and sister cracking up as we pulled up in the driveway. We packed the food and NOW, we were ready to go...and off we went.

Our first stop would be Bakersfield, which was half way to our primary road stop of San Diego. I had made a rule that we would drive no more than 2 to 4 hours each day, stopping frequently, so it would not be just a drive, but be a real vacation with sights all along the way.

San Diego was an important stop. My son's dad and his wife, who were family for my son, still served as important family members to my nephews as well. They had grown up to always consider him, not just an uncle, but an important male influence in their lives.

We stayed at a little place on the beach for a few days. My son and his cousins spent the days with dad and returned to the beach hotel in the evenings with me.

Next day we headed north to the little town of Paris, and the Orange Empire Railway. We rode the train and trolley and since the mercury was going to hit

114 that day, we left by noon. We headed a little further north to catch up with more of our extended Southern California family.

We arrived at the house and upon entering, smelled the aroma of the 'zuga' (Italian slang for spaghetti sauce) and of course the garlic bread. We all sat down to catch up and compare notes. It was a wonderful meal and a nice walk down 'memory lane'.

After dinner we headed back to San Diego for the evening. Again, combining a great railroad experience that day with a great life and family experience, grew my son's world.

After San Diego we were off to Campo to ride another train. We got there in plenty of time to peruse the collection in the museum. We were excited when we were told that during the train trip we would land in a tunnel on the US and Mexico border.

It was equally exciting when the engineer noticed my son and his train knowledge, and invited us all into the cab of the engine. It was great to see my nephews enjoy that added bit of attention thanks to their young cousin's expertise. The train trip was fantastic and the stop at the border part way through the tunnel at the US and Mexico border was a welcome reprieve from the, soon to be, triple digit temperature.

On to Yuma Arizona we went. Not too long a drive, but once over the Colorado River it was miserable. We arrived in triple digit heat and when we pulled up to the hotel I had booked, I understood why the room rate was so low. The place I had reserved had no pool. I thought "Are you kidding me?" For those of you who know me, I obviously left out the 'expletive' in that thought.

I bit the bullet. It was too late to cancel without payment but we found an alternative spot with a pool. To my disappointment I found that, even though there was a pool, the air-conditioning was questionable. Luckily, we were only staying the one night before going on to Phoenix.

In the morning we packed up, took a dive in the pool, hopped in the van, and headed out into the desert. I was trying to save gas since it was at an all time high that year ($5.00/gallon in Southern Cal). We drove as far as we could in our wet swimsuits, on wet towels and with wet hair, to keep cool. About half way to Phoenix we were all dried out and on went the air-conditioning.

We stayed in Phoenix that night and the next morning headed to Flagstaff. Once in Flagstaff I discovered that the world famous Meteor Crater was not that far away. We drove east and took in one of the most interesting places I've ever been to. The guys seconded that opinion!

The next morning while on our way to the next excursion train which was Verde Canyon, we would stop in Sedona. We would also visit the ancient Indian village of Tuzigoot before rolling into Verde Canyon.

The Verde Canyon trip was spectacular and the food and drink for all, was an added bonus. My nephews and I spent a lot of time inside a cab car enjoying the amenities. My son spent most of his time outside in an open car to experience the sights and sounds and smells along the way.

It was back to Flaggstaff that afternoon and as the trip went, we were now heading into the stretch. We were going to the Grand Canyon in the morning, of course by train!

I had booked the observation car which would give us a clear view of the terrain for the entire trip to the rim of the Grand Canyon Railway. We had food, drinks, live music and an unbelievable view as we headed towards the canyon.

It was a steam engine that pulled the train so the sound of the whistle added to the ambiance. Unfortunately the maintenance crew may have partied a little bit too much the night before, and forgot to inspect the bearings. It may not have been their fault, as steam engines can be un-predictable, but we were delayed a bit when the bearings over-heated and we had to stop a bit for the cool down.

Once we got rolling again we still arrived at the canyon rim in time to take in this wonderful site, walk a few trails, and not be late for the return trip.

That night was our last night in Arizona before heading to Las Vegas. I was in the lobby of our hotel looking over the travel brochure rack just in case there was something interesting close by that I may have missed when planning the trip.

There it was... a brochure that detailed the Maverick Helicopters that flew into the Grand Canyon. I hated to fly and had not flown for years due to a bad experience, but I couldn't help thinking what a wonderful opportunity this would be for my nephews.

I gathered the guys and reviewed the information with them. I told them we would have to give up one of the two nights in Vegas to finance this but was not surprised when they jumped at the chance.

Seeing their unbelievable excitement, I was caught up in the moment and didn't think about details. As I regained my sanity at some point, I was also wondering what I was getting them into and how I would deal with my son if he had to give up his final train excursion on the Nevada Southern Railroad.

The next morning we headed to the Maverick complex, went inside, and learned that with a very short wait and a whole lot of cash, these guys could be out flying in a helicopter. I just assumed that there was an age requirement, and my son and I would be waving goodbye to my nephews as they flew out.

Well, stupid me. The rule was that as long as you had an adult with you, you were welcome on board.

Mind you, I hadn't flown for years in a conventional plane and never in a helicopter. My son was looking at me, assuming I would agree to get on a helicopter so he could go as well.

The staff of pilots essentially "shamed me" into taking my son on this journey. They did a great sales job and assured me not one single helicopter had ever gone down.

Pulling out every ounce of 'motherly love' I had, I purchased the tickets for all of us. I would have killed for a shot of 'something' to calm me down, but instead I had that inner talk with myself we all have when we have to "just get through something"...especially for our children.

In walked the cutest kid, wearing a great pilot jacket and a big smile. I thought to myself...."oh, he must be one of the pilot's son's." Think again, I was told he was going to be our pilot.

As we headed out through the door to our vehicle I internally spoke to myself, and under my breath threw enough "F" bombs to last the rest of my life.

Surprisingly, I was told the helicopter would be loaded based on everyone's size and weight. Given this fact, I was also told that I would have to sit right up front next the pilot. Lucky me....

We were all strapped in, rotors whirring, and off we went. With my son the other light-weight passenger in the seat next to me, there was no turning back.

As I looked back at my nephews in the back seat, the sheer size of their smiles immediately convinced me I would have no regrets.

What an amazing 25 minutes in all our lives! We would not only fly to the Canyon rim, scattering elk all along the way, we would actually descend down into this vast canyon and steeply climb out again. With screams, and awe, deserving of the event, we then headed back to the tarmac.

Back on the planet, we were headed to Vegas. Along the way we stopped at this strange little place called Seligman along old route 66. Later we stopped again to see Hoover Dam. It was a great day but we still couldn't stop talking about the helicopter ride.

Pulling into Vegas that afternoon, finding a reasonably priced motel in place of the suite we had given up for the Maverick ride, we were spent. My nephews headed out to the strip for awhile, my son and I packed it in, as we would be venturing out the next morning for one last train excursion.

Next morning it was off to the Nevada Southern Railway. It was another great day for a train ride. We met lots of interesting people, and again my son was in 'all his glory' doing what he loved to do most.

We got back in time to check out and head to the "big surprise" I had in store for my traveling buddies.

As we pulled up to the Bellagio, valet parked and checked in at the front desk again, these guys were all smiles. Our rooms were suites overlooking Las Vegas, and the bathrooms alone were bigger than the bedrooms we had at home.

We were "all dressed up" but definitely had somewhere to go. I had given the staff at the steakhouse a 'heads up' about my little group. They did not disappoint. We were seated right next to the window to enjoy the fountains set to music. We got the seafood platter served so high on a pedestal that it was hard to see each other over the top.

Then, on to a steak that melted in your mouth, and a dessert that would be something you never, ever, had again in your life.

All in all, it was one of those times, one of those trips that simply went "without a hitch". The bills associated with that trip eventually diminished and disappeared over time. The memories are there forever.

Suggestion

If you have a chance to combine your child's passion with other great life experiences… "grab that chance!"

"45"

Chapter 4

Class of 45

When my son was three years old we relocated from our home in Southern California, to my hometown in Northern California. This gave him a chance to be raised around his extended family. Although it was hard on his dad, his dad understood the importance of being raised along- side grandparents, aunts, uncles, and cousins like he and I had been.

Already a train enthusiast, it was our luck that the move put us only a short drive from a world renowned train museum. During the next several years we would enjoy the family gatherings, events, and frequent trips to the train museum on the weekends.

If there was an occasion when his dad or his grandma traveled to see him, it was automatic that a trip to the museum was a given, and he would give them the "grand tour".

He knew every detail of every train at the museum. He knew the history, the specifications, the wheel sets, traction power and anything you could possibly want to know. He impressed not only his family but often engaged the docents in the museum, as he seemed to know as much as they did.

The docents seemed to appreciate this young man and his interest. They would test his knowledge, asking questions he couldn't possibly know the answer to. Surprise...surprise...there were very few questions that he could not answer. In addition he might even go on to add other tidbits of information which they may or may not have known themselves.

Now in high school, although he continued to be a train enthusiast, our trips to the museum were less frequent. We might go down for a special event, but essentially it was not always a part of our plans on a weekend.

One morning, reading the Sunday paper, I saw an announcement that the museum was starting a new Docent training class. I wondered if my son might be interested in this. God knows he had the knowledge about the trains, but would he want to engage with the 'public at large'?

It certainly couldn't hurt to get more details and possibly expand his world and his social interactions so

I called the number and talked to a gal who happened to live in our area. She indicated that the minimum age requirement was eighteen. I let her know my son was only sixteen but that I was certain she would be very surprised with his knowledge.

I asked her if she would at least let him go through the interview process for experience sake. I explained how much time we had spent in the museum over the years and added the fact he had actually driven several trains as a participant in various 'engineer for a day' programs.

Obviously hearing the determination in my voice, she was gracious enough to grant my wish. An interview was scheduled for the upcoming week and although my son had the required attire, it would be his first time creating a resume.

I remember thinking...how the hell do you put together a resume for a sixteen year old? Once we sat down and started listing the milestones in his young life in chronological order, it actually surprised me how much he had done. Keep in mind, it was a Docent Training class, and everything train related was important.

From his first trip on the local river train, handling the throttle and whistle under the supervision of the engineer, to the engineer for a day programs that at the time didn't require a driver's license, he had experience. As long as he was with someone over eighteen he was able to participate.

I took him to the museum on the day of the interview and met the volunteer coordinator in person for the first time. She had a very disarming character, and was quite comfortable with engaging my son in a couple of preliminary questions. She then led him off to the interview room, making sure he understood he would be put through the exact same requirements as any potential Docent.

During what seemed an eternity I began talking myself through a scenario of how I would explain things to him if he was unable to pass the test. I knew the interview process was a good experience for him but maybe also a time when I would have to explain defeat.

I was in the lobby area of the museum waiting. In she came, him a bit behind with a look I found hard to interpret. She walked up to me and said four little words…"When can he start"? There have been very few times, if any, that four little words brought me such joy.

She did indicate that she couldn't give her final approval until she checked on a few details, like the fact no one under eighteen had ever been allowed into the program. She had become a huge fan of our plight, and seemed determined to make this work.

A few days later she called me. She said the proverbial "I have good news and I have bad news". I asked her for the good news first. She stated she had run her request 'up the food chain'. Although the powers that be did approve her request to allow someone younger that 18 to participate, the bad news was that an adult would have to be with him at all times until he met the age requirement.

Of course that adult would be me. I would have to attend the training classes with my son. If he passed, I would be required to be on-site with him each time he volunteered as a Docent.

As she gave me details about the required night classes and Saturday training sessions, it wasn't until a few days later that I began to wonder how we would possibly manage the classes. The classes would be after all day at school for him and after all day at work for me. How would staying out several nights a week, for several weeks, affect our current life?

You might think it was a 'no-brainer' for me, but I did have to seriously consider if making this commitment was sustainable over time. I am of the ilk that once you start something, you have to finish. It was important to teach my son that lesson, but I was fearful that night school and several weekends would be tough for him. How would I handle it if he wanted to quit?

Thinking it through, I realized this museum endeavor was no different than supporting a child who wanted to play soccer or basketball. It required lots of extra time for your child, but for you as a parent as well. You have to get them to practice, still make sure all the school commitments are met, not to mention the impact on family meals and cleaning house.

Forging ahead, classes were to begin in two weeks. We would be there in the evenings and then several Saturdays in order to complete the training.

From the very first night, right through to the end of the sixth week, not once did I regret my decision. Not only was I reminded that my son was energetic about 'all things train' and had no problem driving down to class after dinner, I found the classes to be quite remarkable.

Generally dealing with this train museum meant, not just knowing the facts and figures of the trains, you were also dealing with the history. Being a history buff myself, I truly enjoyed the classes and met some great people.

At the conclusion of the class there would be a graduation ceremony for this group which would now be known as the 'class of 45'. It was a fairly brief event where family and friends were welcome. Each new Docent would be presented with their official engraved gold Museum name badge, along with a parking sticker.

The ceremony was held in the theater with each new docent seated on the stage. The director of the museum spoke of his appreciation for the class, now part of the museum family. He shared with the small group that without volunteers the museum would be impossible to run.

I was so happy when family members as well as a few teachers, past and present, came to the ceremony. We all took our seats and waited for the ceremony to begin. Just then, I noticed that the volunteer coordinator was chatting with my son on stage. He pointed up in my direction and she then walked off the stage and up the stairs towards our group.

She approached me with an envelope and asked me why I was not on stage. I reminded her, this is 'his dream', not mine. He was part of the Class of 45, I was just a willing participant in supporting his dream.

She gave me my envelope, and reminded me that, none the less, I was now a Docent too and she would see me on his first volunteer day.

When his name was called and he walked to the podium for his badge the standing ovation and the 'hoops and hollers' from our group were unmatched. This brought some laughter not only from the Museum staff, but from the entire Class of 45 as well.

So my son was now 'officially' the youngest volunteer ever at the museum. Since our state parks and recreation department ran the museum, he was also now the youngest volunteer for the entire state as well.

From that day forward, and for several years, my son and I would go the museum every other Saturday, first shift, and be Docents for a day. By having a set routine we would become part of the 'regulars' on that day and that shift.

My son becoming a docent meant that not only was he living his passion but he would also be exposed to the general public, the outside world, on a regular basis. This wasn't the safe and somewhat predictable life of school. This wasn't the comfort of home, not having to engage if you so choose. This was out in the world, dealing with people and situations that had to be attended to.

I believe this was the most pivotal point in his life. Everything that came after would be secured and grounded in this experience. Many of his successes would be based on this venture. He was in a world of trains, but more importantly, a world that included a constant supply of information to be processed.

Suggestion

Do what you can...just do what you can...to support your child. Take every opportunity to get them 'out in the world'.
It's not only about the present...it can set the groundwork for the future.

Chapter 5

It's Always a Good Day at the Museum

After the Docent graduation my son and I were free to volunteer at any time that suited us. Due to school and work it looked like Saturday mornings for the first shift would suit us best.

I'm not easily intimidated, but I will admit, I was intimidated the first few times we arrived at the museum. We were required to sign in at the Docent lounge and report to the station master. When we arrived in the lounge on our first Saturday morning it was clear that my son and I were the only "newbie's" that day. I wondered where our classmates were.

Surely at least a few would have shown up?

We signed the roster and took a position off to the side. Everyone in the room seemed very comfortable with the routine, a routine we would eventually come to know. But on that day we were clearly somewhat of a surprise to the group. Some greeted us and some merely stared as they waited for the station master to begin the morning meeting.

Rather than a single station master, we had the luxury of having two station masters for the Saturday morning line up. Apparently these two guys drove in together, and always made sure all the assignments were covered for the day. If we were short of staff, one of these two would act as station master while the other might cover a vacant assignment.

The group in the lounge, far beyond my son's age, and mine as well, all seemed to know each other very well. They were obviously engaging in their customary routine, all fully aware of what their assignments would be. I tried to respect their routine but we had been told that as long as we signed up in advance on the calendar for an assignment, it was ours.

It became painfully clear that the assignments we had signed up for typically belonged to some of the experts that were now in the room. These experts weren't used to having to sign up for an assignment it was just 'understood' the area they would cover.

The station masters, trying to keep things

'politically correct', struggled with how they would announce the plans for the morning shift. What would typically be 'understood' now had to be adjusted to accommodate others in the room, namely, my son and me.

So now, on our very first day, we had already stepped on some toes. My son had signed up for one of the most popular spots for all these railroad guys, the cab forward. I had signed up for the mail car, an exhibit that was manned on a regular basis by a gentleman who actually worked on the car 'back in the day'.

Thank God I didn't know this at the time. I would have been mortified knowing I had taken this coveted spot from a true expert.

In their defense, they had seen hundreds of new docents come and go, very few becoming a part of the regular volunteer staff. Spending a whole lot of time and energy on new recruits wasn't always time well spent.

I can't say they were exactly "gracious" that first day, but they did acknowledge our presence. Although skeptical about allowing us to work in the assignments we had signed up for, they knew that according to the rules, if someone had put their name on an open assignment it was theirs for the keeping.

We completed our check-in and went off to the morning meeting with the Museum staff. This was quite a different scenario. Not only were we introduced and 'welcomed' by the staff, there were other docents, who we had not previously met while in the lounge, who introduced themselves and offered any assistance we might need on this, our first day.

This meeting included updates and news about the museum and announcements were made regarding special groups or events we could expect that day. Attending that morning meeting was a police officer and his partner 'Thor'.

Thor was a police dog who specialized in bomb sniffing. It was post 9/11 and the museum had to be "cleared" by Thor before opening the museum to the public. At the time I'm not sure I felt safer once the area had been cleared, or less safe, because it had to be done in the first place. These are things we would all struggle with for years to come.

Meeting closed, everyone with their marching orders, it was opening time at the museum. As we walked off to our assignments I wondered how the day would go. I wondered how my son would do, and what the staff and visitors would think of him.

After being checked on a few times, and having brief chats with the station masters, I thought things were going well. My son and I were obviously being monitored, but it was for the good of the museum visitors. Staff was making sure we were performing our duties and that was their job.

I noticed that part way into the shift both station masters were heading out together for lunch. I wondered at the time "who would be in charge?" I also came to realize that on their watch, they made sure everything was taken care of, the museum staff was on board, and then, and only then would they enjoy their well deserved lunch hour. It was a rule.

Now I got it! The routines were not because of strict adherence to some pre-designed preferences of existing staff, they were designed to assure everything would go as smoothly as possible for the visitors regardless of the staff and docents present that day.

I backed up a bit, had my son back up a bit, and decided that for the time being, we would sign up for 'floor' positions. This gave us the opportunity to spend time with each docent, in each exhibit, and learn from the 'pros'.

I recognized that these docents, even though they loved to be around younger folks, weren't use to being around a youngster who was a fellow docent. They were working outside their comfort zone but did all they could to include my son. I will always respect and cherish them for that.

As we continued to show up every other Saturday morning without fail, we gained their trust and they realized we were in it "for the long haul". We also learned that at times we would need to adjust to the needs of the team. This meant we might not always be in the position we had signed up for.

My son, being a rules oriented, literal thinker, at first didn't understand why a station master might ask him to cover a position he had not signed up for. I was the one who had urged my son into the floor position to give breaks and learn from others, so this put him in a difficult position.

On one occasion when the station master asked him to spend time in a train car he was not as familiar with, or fond of, he stated "I signed up for the floor". He wasn't being rude, just stating a fact.

It was years later that I found out that a very 'astute' volunteer had been quietly monitoring our situation from behind the scenes. She was a lady who embodied the museum, who understood what it was, and what it was supposed to be.

She may have been front and center, obviously putting in her time at the museum, but she also worked behind the scenes, no 'kudos' necessary, as she went about her tasks, making sure things that needed to be taken care of, were in fact, taken care of.

She obviously must have understood my purpose. She recognized that rather than just dropping him off, I was there and willing to do the work necessary to make sure, not only was he comfortable, but that the existing staff at the museum, were comfortable as well. Much more than that, she understood my son. She felt he deserved to be there as much as anyone.

She had noticed our strict adherence to Saturdays. When one of the station masters complained to her that we were not flexible when asked to alter our assignments, she stepped up big time.

She pointed out that given the rules and that my son was a rule oriented kind of guy, they had to be the ones to adjust. She let them know, in no uncertain terms, they would need to help him learn over time to make these adjustments as a 'team player'.

It didn't take too long. If my son was asked to take an assignment unexpectedly he was happy to do so. They on the other hand did everything in their power to have him cover the spot he had signed up for.

In this big new world of the museum, my son was always anxious and excited to talk to the other docents about "all things trains". He was finally in a place where his vast knowledge seemed welcomed, and the folks he was talking to understood him.

As a young child, no more than four feet tall, when he engaged a person at a train outing or event, given his age and size, people were quite impressed and entertained by his knowledge. He was positively reinforced to chatter on about the subject on tap, namely trains.

Now that he was older, I'm sure a few of the docents figured he was trying to show off, and was trying to 'one-up' them with his knowledge. Once they got to know him they realized, he was just excited to finally be in a place where he could communicate with people who shared his interest. Even better, that they understood what he was talking about and had comments of their own.

Over the next several years we were part of the 'regular' Saturday crew at the museum. We showed up religiously for the first shift, always checking in to confirm where we might be needed that day regardless of the assignment we had signed up for. These were very happy times for both of us.

He would report as needed to his assignment...I would disappear off to my own assignment. These years were so important, as he was independent and functioning in his own right. Although I might be the one getting him to the museum in the morning, and be part of the morning meetings, after that, he was on his own to interact with the visitors and fellow docents.

In this world he was a regular person. He was now a thriving young man in a world surrounded by older gentleman that could teach him things. Even though there was a disparity in their ages, he now had 'peers' as part of a group that came together for a single purpose.

Before his time as a docent it was family interactions that helped shape him. I will add, they did an outstanding job! Being part of my family, and his dad's family, he felt accepted and was always excited to engage with them.

Now, moving out into the world, it was the staff and fellow volunteers at the museum that helped shape his confidence. Not only did he continue to grow 'physically' during these years but socially and emotionally his maturity level exploded!

In the museum environment he, like the other docents, was the "go to guy" for information. He had the answers to most all of the questions the visitors might have. He, like all the other docents would be fully prepared to answer the most asked question of all...."Where are the bathrooms?"

Each time, on our drive home I would ask him about his day. We would chat a bit about the day and compare notes about the people we talked to. I might pass along that I had met people from another country, or who spoke a different language, he might share that he had met up with someone who had new information on one of the trains.

All in all, it was 'always' a good day at the museum.

Suggestion

Help your child adjust to the world. It will help the world adjust to your child.

Chapter 6

Dust Bunnies

I am continually amazed that often it's the smallest things, those seemingly insignificant occurrences, that lead to big leaps in one's thinking, or one's life. In this dust bunnies were the "something small" that would make a big difference.

I had always made sure my son had chores and responsibilities around the house. They would be age appropriate and I did not pay for the services. These tasks were an expectation, a part of being an active member of the household.

I felt that participating in the mundane chores around the house gave him a sense of pride in his contribution. From feeding the pets, to taking out the trash, to making the bed each morning, all of his responsibilities would help him grow.

During his summer break I would ask him to complete tasks around the house. I would always follow-up with leaving a short list of the things he needed to accomplish by the time I arrived at home that day. Leaving a written list was very important as it reminded him what needed to be done. It not only helped him to be clear about what needed to be done, it also eliminated any excuse that he had "forgotten".

I explained to him that getting these things done during the week it would free up time for things like the museum on a Saturday, or a trip to the State Fair when it was running.

When I arrived at home I was never disappointed, as the listed assignments were always completed. If it wasn't done quite up to my standards, as an obsessive-compulsive person, I would wait until he was out of the area and go behind to make it 'perfect'. I didn't want him to think that he hadn't done a good job as that would defeat the whole purpose of the assignment.

Over time this continued to be our routine. It was working out quite well and as he aged the list would get a bit longer, but never too long to cut into a well deserved summer break.

One day I arrived at home noting that one of his tasks was to vacuum the kitchen floor. We had a dog, and still do, that sheds not in tiny little hairs, but rather in large furry sorts of light weight hair balls. These balls of fur distinctly resemble the dust bunnies we discover when we haven't cleaned behind the refrigerator for some time.

That day the canine 'dust bunnies' were readily visible in the corners of the kitchen. Normally I would simply wait for him to involve himself in some task and pick up the dust bunnies myself. On that day I was taken aback that he had not noticed them himself. I wondered when was the last time I had taken him for an eye exam?

Before calling him in and acting like some sort of drill sergeant, I realized that by going behind him and 'fixing' things even when it was age appropriate, I had somehow lost track of time. At this point he was more than ready to move on, step-up his game, and perform tasks of higher quality. I was the one at fault for not revisiting the things that I clearly needed to teach him.

This was not the time to ask him a question like "do you see that?" His answer would be most assuredly be 'yes' and that would be that. The inference of something more, something he might pick up on, in terms of what I meant, would be lost on him.

This was not the time to suddenly, out of nowhere, show any amount of disappointment that he had not done something properly. After all, he was just doing what he was always expected to do, and further, always thanked for it.

It was time for a teaching moment. One that would result in higher quality performance but more importantly, continue to instill the pride I wanted him to have in himself, for a job well done.

I had been remiss in teaching my son how to do certain tasks. I was now sticking to my core principles that if we spend time teaching, and asking a person to give the best they have to offer, the pride and self-esteem will come.

We can't all get first place, but we can work as hard as we can, to do the best that we can. If we get a trophy or 'kudos' for minimal effort I'm not sure we will learn any sense of working harder for the better results that could likely come. This was the era when the new thinking was "everybody gets a trophy". If everyone gets a trophy I believe the value of the trophy is greatly diminished.

I asked him to grab the vacuum cleaner, so I could show him something new. He brought in the machine and I showed him the attachments that could be used for certain types of work. We went over the tubes and the various configurations of the items positioned on the arm of the vacuum.

I had him remove the tube and attach the thin tool, then used the 'dust bunnies' in the corner as an example of the types of things these tools were designed to take care of. He happily used these new tools to vacuum up all the dust bunnies in the corners.

I further explained that in the future, once he was done with the vacuuming, he should take another look at anything that might require these new tools to fully remove them from the floor.

Now we had conquered the kitchen floor. But it caused me to look at any and all things I had failed to move forward with from the "dark ages". I realized that even though routines and predictability had such a huge and calming effect on our lives, I would need to be more diligent in monitoring when it was time to change those routines.

Whenever I thought it might be time to take things to a new level I would have to go back to our roots, and make sure things were clearly taught and discussed before putting them into place. I had to remember that my son didn't always absorb learning from what was going on around him. He responded much better if things were clearly defined, discussed, and practiced.

Once he had learned something, the beauty was, he never forgot. Once he was clear on what was expected, he never failed. God love the 'literal thinker'.

I didn't have to listen to the ridiculous whining of a teenager who feigned 'forget-fullness' when they clearly were just too caught up in themselves. I didn't have to listen to the inane comments and explanations for why something wasn't done.

Out in the 'real world' there are not too many bosses who allow forgetfulness as an excuse for not getting something done. I think that by being clear on expectations, and my son being receptive to that, he had a much better chance of performing in the future.

Now, thanks to those little dust bunnies, I was more observant and more proactive in looking for signs that my son was maturing and could take things to a higher level.

Suggestion
Don't make random requests….Set expectations that are predictable for your child. Most of all…Watch for opportunities to take your child to the next level in an informative and positive way.

Chapter 7

A Carefree Summer…"Indeed"

    As the summer approached I was not quite ready to leave my son at home all day while I was at work. He was well past the age for childcare so I reached out to friends and colleagues who knew our situation.

    I was looking for a responsible and reliable person who needed a summer job and was willing to work for a reasonable wage. I was also interested in finding a young person who would welcome the opportunity to hang out with a pretty interesting character…namely, my son.

Low and behold, one of my colleagues knew a young man, one he had known for years, the son of his good friend. This young man was home from college just for the summer and wanted to make a few bucks. When he heard about my situation, he jumped at the chance.

He was highly intelligent, had Eagle Scout credentials, and was home from Massachusetts Institute of Technology (MIT), for the summer. It doesn't get any better than that.

I invited him to the house for an interview and, of course, to meet my son. This ended up being 'easy...squeezy'...and was going to work out just fine for all of us.

During the interview I noticed that he seemed a bit distracted by the Nintendo set-up my son had left out in front of the TV. He began asking my son questions about the set-up, and the various games in his inventory. I thought it was a very nice touch, already establishing a comradeship with my son in advance.

We talked about the starting date and daily routine. As he left I felt this would likely go well. I would later look back and think I had no idea how really well it would go. This young man's name was Will even though it was for a short run, I doubt whether we would forget him any time soon.

As Will left I asked my son how he felt about Will coming over each day. I asked him "would you like that?"...he answered "indeed". Will, being quite taken aback by this phrase, a 'catch phrase' my son had picked up from reading the British versions of train books, I also asked Will..."will you like coming over each day?" He in turn answered 'indeed'.

The summer rolled out and each day I returned from work to two young men, apparently quite pleased with their new accomplishments on Nintendo 64. I was actually surprised that Will was so engaged in this. Nintendo was at the time, an outdated game. I wondered if he was just being a responsible individual, assuring my son had the opportunity to keep busy doing something he enjoyed, or whether he was actually enjoying the challenges as well.

What I discovered was that Nintendo 64, an 'ancient' game by technology standards, was making a come-back with college age kids. The controllers and game packs were hard to find so Will was very happy to have fallen upon a treasure trove of equipment and so many games.

Years before I had purchased the equipment and one of the few games available, 'Super Mario'. My son and I, not communicating much, could sit and play this game together, making a connection that was lots of fun. I actually became quite intrigued with the game. Although my son became very good at the game fairly quickly, I eventually caught up and was very serious about my 'Star' earnings as well.

At that time my mom was often picking up my son from school and bringing him home until I arrived. She also got interested in some of the new games we were purchasing and became fairly hooked on "Cruising USA". This was a car challenge that involved racing your opponent, but also had a time trial series.

My mom, being quite the fast driver, but a good driver as well, seemed to love challenging herself to faster and faster times. I remember one time coming to the front door, letting myself in, just to find her in front of the TV in a near state of panic. I think she thought I would interrupt her game, but I stayed silent.

My son was rooting her on and it appeared she was beating a new record that would literally, on this game, "take her to the moon".

That being said, time passed and daily life would change. Other interests would take over, and the Nintendo 64 console, controllers, and games were tucked away.

One Christmas our family 'adopted' a family in need and the Nintendo inventory was a perfect gift for the kids who had very little. We gave them the console, the controllers and all the games we had acquired over time. Our life was full, but "Nintendo-Less".

Time passed again and there would be a renewed interest in Nintendo 64 since the graphics had yet to be copied. I took my son down to a used video store where we once again purchased a Nintendo 64 set-up, albeit used. We re-built our inventory of games and actually started enjoying time together once again engaged in a single activity.

    Enter Will. Unbeknownst to me, the Nintendo 64 had made a come-back, to the college age crowd. They were in the Xbox age...sports games, war games and more violent type of game playing. They were too young to be familiar with Nintendo 64 but had now re-discovered this old game.

    Now, rediscovered, the Nintendo 64 was interesting to them as it took lots of skill, had great graphics, and unless you purchased the "cheat book" it was very hard to figure out.

    So, during that summer, my son would be Will's 'go to guy' on how to become an expert at Nintendo. He would then return to MIT, a virtual super star. When you talk about 'win-win'...this was 'textbook'.

    When I arrived each day from work, sometimes Will had a vehicle, some days we would drive him the short distance to his home. I would often overhear a few conversations and without fail....I became aware that Will had picked up the catch phrase 'indeed'...from my son.

    Later, when I asked my son about his summer with Will, he said, "it was the most carefree summer I ever had". This answer told me that he felt he was not being "watched over" but was actually just hanging out, feeling safe, doing something with someone who valued him.

    I have since learned that Will graduated from MIT and is now at NASA. No surprise. But I often wonder, if he was asked something like "do you love your job?" What would he answer? I'm betting…"Indeed"

Suggestion
If you aren't quite ready to leave them on their own….seek out alternatives with individuals that are closer to their age.

Chapter 8

The Girl from Ipanema

Over my long years of employment I met so many people I enjoyed working with, but no one more than Miss 'P'. She had a beautiful face to match her beautiful name but to me she was always just Miss 'P'.

I don't mean to imply this is my name for her, in an effort to keep her anonymity this is really what I called her. Later, as we became friends, and still are to this day, I simply call her, 'P'.

She is the type of young woman who has the endearing quality of not really noticing how much she impresses the people around her. I would watch her work, seeing people around noticing her efforts to go above and beyond, but to her it is just "what she does".

There's something very special...about a person who doesn't realize they are special.

When she walked down a hallway and stopped to chat with a person or a group of people, her disarming personality always served as a positive experience for everyone. I loved to see her continue down the hall, on her way back to work, never noticing that the guys always looked back in her direction, to get that final 'glimpse' of this oh so pretty girl.

It reminded me of a long lost song..."The Girl from Ipanema". A song that described a beautiful girl walking along the beach and never noticing as she walked on by...the boys said "AAAHHHH". (YouTube it)

We had worked together occasionally but it wasn't until a new unit opened at the hospital that I was able to convince her to come over to "my side of the hall way". We both spent the days fulfilling all our duties, but in the process had an opportunity to chat while we worked.

During those chats, as we got to know each other better, we discussed our boys. I with the one boy shared the stories of the things going on in our lives at the time. She with her two boys, had lots of stories to tell as well. We both liked to laugh a lot. Most of our stories were centered on sharing an experience that brought about a sense of joy and laughter and how life was rolling out in a positive, although somewhat quirky, sort of way. A lot of our stories ended in the statement..."REALLY"....as it was stated on both sides of the fence.

I might tell a funny story about an unusual occurrence, and because of our understanding of each other, I would look at her, feigning disappointment but say "really"..."is this what I signed up for?" She would laugh like hell.

She too could say something like "oh guess what happened yesterday"? Then proceed to tell the story, and with a smirk...say "I mean really?"...."can you believe it?"...and I would in turn laugh like hell.

One day as we were working together on a project, having one of our 'chats' she seemed to want to share a bit of information on a concern she had. Not something funny, but something that had come up.

She, in listening to my tales, had come to realize that maybe the issues that were coming up with her son were something she should take a bit more seriously. We started to chat about her boy in more detail. As he grew older she was concerned about his future.

I described to her how the school system had approached me years before and indicated I might want to look into a few things. As hard as it was at the time I knew it was something I needed to do. At this early stage by taking him to a few doc's and specialists I was able to get the documentation that he and I would eventually need years later.

My son was so young at the time that I doubt he even remembers anything. For me, the tough part was getting a written report on what was 'suspected'. This would serve him well and left no scar.

My son being on an Individual Education Plan (IEP) through elementary, middle school, and now in high school, triggered a process that would again serve him well if he wanted to proceed to college or work, post high school.

I always made sure my son was at every IEP meeting. It was critical to me that everything was 'up-front' and that he understood, and had input into what was going on. I know this made him feel somewhat uncomfortable at an older age, having come to realize things weren't perfect but it was the right thing to do.

I always explained to him that nothing was "wrong", he just needed support in areas that he struggled with. He had asked me questions on what 'Asperger's' meant. I explained to him that he was exceptionally smart, exceptionally special, and therefore had to deal with issues not everyone would have to deal with. Later, he would boldly recognize, in his own words, that he knew he had Asperger's, but "had grown out of it".

For my Miss 'P', having lots of family support and an undeniable sense of responsibility and resilience, her son had made it through so many mile-stones. This made it difficult for her to admit that she may have to intervene, and come up with a new plan.

As she cried that day, knowing she was again moving towards new territory, I explained that in my son's early years in high school I was approached to discuss what would happen "after" graduation. After dealing with the early years, the middle years, and now, him doing very well in high school, I remembered that back then I thought that if I just kept on course, everything would continue to work out well. She was in that same place now.

I don't quite remember who it was, but at one of our IEP meetings I was gently reminded that there were lots of programs, post high school, might benefit my son. I remember a comment that resonated with me. It was to the point, and made a lot of sense. If there were services available, that didn't always mean you had to partake of them. If my child could benefit from any of the services, if I didn't set them up now that ship would sail. It would be too late to access resources that he may possibly need in the future.

I got the meaning loud and clear. Even though he was barely ready to start his sophomore year, it was time to start planning for the future.

Luckily I had covered the bases of reports, paperwork and other necessities of the 'system' early on.

Like me, Miss P had been so extraordinarily successful at raising her son to a high level of performance, it never occurred to her what might happen when the world got bigger, got a bit tougher, and more unpredictable.

She regrouped, as she always did, and started down the path of getting that oh-so important diagnosis. That oh-so important paperwork, detailing things that were hard to chew on, but understanding it needed to be done to assure her son had every opportunity.

I'm sure it was hard on her son as he was of an age that he would clearly have to process the thought that something might be "wrong". Always feeling deeply for her child, Miss P had to process the same. I'm just glad we had the talk and that I was able to offer the gift of 'experience'.

We went through the steps together. I had stepped and mis-stepped a few times so I was able to give her some good advice.

I was so thankful that my son had a 'plan' in place for post high school, in this case college, where he could access services that would support him. The high school team on his side would help him navigate the entry requirements and orientation that would ultimately help him seamlessly move on.

It was also rewarding to have now passed this information on to someone who could benefit, not to mention someone I cared deeply about.

The more you plan in advance, giving your child a sense that they are simply "moving on", the better the experience it will be. You can't wait until "after" high school to decide what happens next.

Eventually my son would move on to a local community college that had a great program to support him as necessary. Her son, a few years younger, would eventually move on to the same college to experience just the same.

During those few years we talked a lot, compared notes, and "laughed our asses off". We shared information that made us both happy, and thankful, that we had taken that 'extra' step to assure our boys were on the right track post-high school.

Funny thing happened one day. I was at the college, waiting to pick up my son at a designated spot. Low and behold there was this nice looking kid, clearly waiting for 'his' ride. He looked so familiar, and I rolled down the window to say hello. You guessed it ...it was 'P's' son.

I called her that day and she indicated he hadn't mentioned it. No surprise there...It was like the day her son was down at the rail station next to the campus, and ran into my son, but they couldn't quite remember how they knew each other. Oh gee....we compared notes and laughed like a couple of 'fools', knowing our bond would likely survive the next several years, if for no other reason than interest in how the story would turn out.

Suggestion

It's never too soon to put a plan in place that will provide the predictability they need. Signing up for services doesn't mean you have to use them. But if you do have to use them, it pays off to have everything in place as early as possible.

Chapter 9

Senior Ball

Late into my son's junior year in high school he suddenly announced that he was interested in attending his junior prom. His interest in attending the prom told me he must have felt comfortable and happy in his environment at school. Naturally I wanted to do what I could to support that.

Unfortunately what I also learned was that the prom was scheduled for the upcoming weekend. Good God, he was so used to me pulling things off, I doubt he understood all the necessary steps and all the arrangements that had to be made. Arrangements such as formal attire, transportation, dinner reservations etc…

This ended up being a key learning experience for him. As mighty as I was, I did not have the where-with-all to get something together so quickly. Apparently his buddy's mom was put in the same position and I contacted her to compare notes.

We both agreed that this would be a teaching moment for both our son's. Since it was far too late to make appropriate arrangements, both boys would learn that their failure to communicate and plan ahead would result in a 'no-go' on the prom.

Disappointed myself, I communicated to my son the reasons behind my inability to support his desire to attend the prom. I made it clear to him that he had to tell me things further in advance if it required my support such as transportation or attire.

When his senior year began he and his buddy realized they would have to be more up front and more diligent if they wanted to attend the senior ball. If they wanted to attend this event they realized it was up to them to share as much information as possible, as much in advance as possible. Apparently we had made our point.

The moment the date for the senior ball was announced my son immediately let me know. I now had literally months to prepare, and sort out how to get him there. This was his next step, and mine too, into realizing that although I was always ready to support him and his plans …he now had reached an age where it was up to him to communicate important information.

Back in my day the Senior Ball had a strict code of 'couples only'. If a girl didn't get asked, or if the guys didn't reach out to a girl and convince her to go, you just didn't attend.

Thank goodness, times had changed. Now anyone who wanted to attend the Senior Ball was welcome to attend. You could come alone, or with a date, or a friend, or with a group of friends.

He was old enough, but still not always sharing details about his day at school. He wouldn't necessarily let me know about the kids he might talk to, or what they would talk about. This was not the time to assume he would get together with a group, or put together a plan that would get him to Senior Ball without my support.

As I reached out to determine what would allow me to support my son's wishes to attend the Senior Ball, it also occurred to me that for him to go 'in style', I would need to network with other parents.

Not knowing where to start in the planning, I decided to reach out to the home room teacher, the strategies coordinator, and to anyone who might help me navigate the complexities of my son's senior year activities.

Speaking to the teachers and his counselor, their suggestion was that I hook up with a few other parents.

I gave them my phone information and hoped they would pass it along to all interested parties so we could start putting together a plan.

Still having an ample amount of time we networked via phone to come up with a reasonably sized group of guys and gals that were interested in going to the Ball. Now with the group put together, all the parents would share in the plan for a dinner and transportation that would give our kids a great experience without 'breaking the bank'.

As the Senior Ball approached it was exciting to arrange for my son's tux and make dinner reservations for that night. It was clearly an opportunity for him to get out and enjoy all the "trappings" of being a senior in high school. Not to mention an opportunity to be out, without his mom, for a change.

On the night of the Senior Ball, as we got our kids to the chosen restaurant, while the kids had their meal, the parents, including me, retreated to the bar for a glass of wine and a bit of food. This was an opportunity for me to discuss my trepidation and nervousness with a group of parents who understood exactly where I was coming from.

We shared funny stories about our preparation for the Ball. We all patted each other's hands to assure each other it was the right thing to do, and that everything would work out fine. As the limo arrived, and as the kids fled to the parking lot, music blaring coming from this limo bus, a good friend of one of the families ready to "take them to the ball" greeted all of us.

I can't accurately, in any way, describe the smiles, or the excitement I saw in those kids' faces at that moment as they hurried towards the limo to board. Any fears I had, any doubts I had, totally disappeared.

The evening rolled on and I kept myself busy, cleaning the house, in an effort to fight off the demons of worry. Eventually my son appeared at the door, with a smile that would last well into the following week. He was safe, and full of new thoughts and new memories to ponder.

As I asked him about the Ball over the next few days, he was more than willing to describe what went on. This was new for me, and I really understood how major events at this age would lead him to communicate more. It would give him the opportunity to describe something really exciting...reliving the moments, and sharing them with me.

Suggestion

If your child shows interest in a social event, network with the school and other parents. There might be other kids out there who deserve the same opportunity.

Chapter 10

Getting Past Q & A (What Happened First, Second, Third)

When we pick up our kids from school, when our spouse walks through the door, when we meet up with our family or friends, naturally we talk, we catch up. This is often preceded by the question "How was your day?"

When we ask this question we 'imply' we are looking for details about how the day rolled out. This question is usually answered with a detailed description of small things, but may also include significant events.

When you ask these kids "How was your day?" their answer will most likely be "Good". That's it. If you ask "What was the best thing about your day?" the answer may be, as in my case, "Everything."

What you are probably looking for is a 'run down' of what happened during the day…right? You don't get the 'run down' so the Q and A begins. Trying to ferret out the events of the day becomes a litany of questions from you, followed by answers from them in the form of disconnected facts and events that almost never follows a logical sequence.

The 'coup de gras' comes hours or sometimes even days later when they blurt out some sort of fairly important, or really important, information they did not share earlier. Out of context and out of sequence they've finally processed and decided to share information. Goody for them, not so 'goody' for you.

There you are, astounded, surprised and semi-frustrated or even angry that the information was not shared earlier. For them it's just something that popped in their heads that moment and they finally decided it's something important enough to share.

In the early years of elementary school you will hopefully be lucky, like I was, to have support from the teachers. These are teachers who would send notes, or even call, to let you know about an important assignment or an important event like a field trip. Maybe a pot-luck and your child had to bring a dish.

Maybe an award ceremony and they were receiving an award. However, you found out from your child the night before, or even the morning of, as almost an afterthought.

Connect with the teachers! It will save you. I remember my son asking in elementary school, "How come every time you come to my school assemblies, I get an award?" I laughed off and on for hours.

The one that stands out for me was an award ceremony at my son's high school. There was a notice sent out giving the date and time of the event. I assumed the notice was just to give us a 'heads up' in case my son or I would like to attend. I had no idea he was sent this invitation because he would be a recipient. I found out quite by accident, luckily running into Mr. Lee that day when I picked up my son, as he said ..."See you tonight". I gave this some thought and asked my son if we should be attending the event.

My son quite 'nonchalantly' announced that according to Mr. Lee he should attend, as he would be receiving an award. I wanted to say "Gee...thanks for letting me know"...but I held my tongue, not wanting to ruin the moment.

That night we went to the awards ceremony. At one point during the ceremony my son's ceramics teacher was introduced to present an art award. This teacher had attended my son's teacher conferences and always seemed interested in my son's progress. We had the beautiful ceramics work my son had done under his watch scattered around the house in aesthetically appropriate places.

This teacher's 'catch-phrase', according to my son, was "right-on". I remembered hearing that catch phrase during the school conferences he attended with us. This was quite an old phrase, even for my time, but it seemed to suit him well. For some un-known reason I was so overwhelmed with emotion, that when this teacher was introduced and as the crowd cheered, I felt the compelling need to stand and shout "right-on!", which I did.

Unfortunately the crowd had finished clapping and were seating themselves by the time my resounding voice announced this phrase. Fortunately most everyone in the crowd, including this teacher, understood the outburst. They laughed quietly and clapped a bit. As I slinked back into my seat, avoiding eye contact with those around me, the ceremonies continued.

Alongside his buddy, my son was now recognized by Mr. Lee as one of two of the hardest working students in his program. The other hard working student was of course the buddy alongside him. They were both stand out students so he couldn't narrow his decision down to just one of them. He announced that both my son and his buddy would both receive the award for outstanding achievement.

As I sat next to his buddy's mom we both welled up with tears…but we also both laughed out loud as a result of our joy.

It was a great moment but I knew I had to focus on how I could get my son to share information without being asked. There was still work to be done. If I was going to support him, I needed to know the details of things, especially if they were important.

On his weekly talks with his Dad I'm sure it would help as well. I'm sure that the Q & A on a phone conversation must have been even more frustrating than what I was dealing with. Anything I could do to help him understand the interest his dad and I had about 'detail' would be my next goal.

I got busy formulating a technique to help my son understand the importance of sharing information without being asked. Just as importantly, I needed to get him to explain the sequence of events when sharing that information, so it made sense.

First, I referred back to previous wins. I told him clearly what he needed to do, whether he knew why or not. I quit asking "How was your day" and instead I asked, "What happened first today"? Then what happened next. Then what happened after that…etc,etc..

I could tell he still had no idea why I even cared about the events of his day, but I persevered. I would ask daily, and as time went on, he started getting a bit frustrated. When he got frustrated enough I simply explained that if he offered what happened first, and then second, and then third I would quit asking him. He now knew if he shared the information up front, in order, the questions would stop.

This worked, and I'm sure it worked if for no other reason, than it would 'shut me up'. Just like in his early years, I quit analyzing why something worked or not, I just kept trying techniques that resulted in positive outcomes.

From then on, for the most part, he describes his day like anyone would. Every now and again I have to remind him the information makes no sense…then he rephrases. When I picked him up from school or from an event, I quit urging him to share information but stayed silent more than a normal amount of time after I greeted him by simply saying "Hello". At some point it occurred to him I was waiting for a description of his day without being asked.

To this day when I say "How was your day?" he makes a point to describe his day in logical sequence and understands this question but more importantly what it 'implies'. He came to understand that I did not want a simple answer of good or bad, but that I was looking for, and interested in, a description of his day.

I felt this skill was very important in his day to day communications with not only me, but with others. This was significant progress towards his understanding of not just literally answering a question, but understanding what that question 'implied'. That expanding knowledge and more critical thinking of what others might expect made him much more successful. He also came to realize that the bits and pieces of his life were in fact important to other people who surrounded him. That is always a good feeling for any of us.

Suggestion

Always remember to describe "literally" your expectation and feel comfortable with "softly" demanding certain things. It will help them expand their communication skills which will serve them practically, but also emotionally, as they interact with the world.

Chapter 11

Harvest Moon

My son made it through high school with flying colors! Not that we had much doubt, but it was great when all the family gathered to celebrate his achievement and put any doubts to rest.

He was now a high school grad, Docent at the museum, and moving on to college. Quite differently from the last several years, he would not be returning to high school in a few months, seeing his friends, acquaintances, and the teachers he was accustomed to seeing.

He would be moving on to new territory, as would I. He was secure in the plan to attend college, but quite frankly neither of us knew what that would look like. This was actually when 'ignorance is bliss'.

College was a go...thanks to the support and planning that was done in the last few years of high school. It was exciting to anticipate new experiences. However, with no knowledge of how the day would look there was no need to worry or get anxious until the time came.

During his high school years he had been much more on his own, but I still always knew where he was and was secure that he was in a safe environment, with lots of folks 'in charge'.

I stuffed away the thoughts away about how I would feel when I dropped him off at the curb on his first day of college, having no clue what would go on. Unlike in kindergarten, where I could semi-stalk him without him noticing, he was going to be truly and completely on his own.

He was boarding a train on his way down the track of life, and all I could do was trust that I had prepared him. He knew his schedule and class locations, and had a cell phone to get in touch if he needed to.

On his first day he was fine. I was the 'basket case'. I got up at the crack of dawn, went to work for a few hours, back home to transport him to his new college, and back to work to complete the day. This would be our new daily life schedule.

He had a bit of a wait before I could pick him up after his last class. As luck would have it, the college campus he chose happened to sit immediately next to a train rail line. Oh gee, lucky again. If he had time to kill before I got there he could simply 'hang out' at the rail station and keep occupied. I would call him when I arrived and we would head home.

This local community college was one of very few colleges in the country that actually offered a program in Railroad Operations. That was a no-brainer for my son. He would take basic college course requirements offered during the day, but would also begin his core courses in railroad operations right out of the gate.

This program was designed to accommodate students who would likely be older, working days, so these core courses were offered only at night. This would have a profound effect on our daily lives for the next few years.

The courses were 'successive', which meant each course was a pre-requisite for the next course. You couldn't double up and take multiple classes in the same semester. So, although it seemed my son was taking a whole lot of time just getting through community college, when you reviewed the curriculum, it was a minimum commitment of at least three years no matter how you looked at it.

By day, he would attend classes on campus, as I went to work. By night, after dinner we would head out for his Railroad Op's classes. Besides being night classes, they were also classes held at an off-site location. Nearly 40 minutes from our home, each way…Oh gee, not so lucky this time.

I knew this would be a major challenge to our normal routine but in his inimitable way, anything that had to do with his passion for trains would be welcomed and not even closely resemble a challenge for him. I knew that embracing his passion would help him accomplish other important things in life, so I accepted that normal routine was now 'out the door'.

I was no 'martyr'. I was just like any other parent who had to get a kid to football practice or a soccer game. We do what we can to make sure our child has opportunities for positive experiences. The time we spend pays off when our child goes out into the world with a solid foundation for surviving.

During the first week I got him to his class but had to determine what I would do during those hours he was occupied. It was way too far to go back home, and come back, but also this was an area where you wouldn't necessarily want to 'hang out' with the local crowd.

Being an avid reader, I would take along my latest novel and enjoy catching up with the story. In the beginning the weather was great and I could sit outside for a bit. After darkness sneaked up, I found an area inside the building where I could pull up a chair and continue my book until his class was over.

I tried to stay away from any mainstream activity as other class members arrived, not wanting to embarrass him. He was what I thought was at that wonderful stage when, in public, teenagers are mortified if they are even within one square mile of a parent.

But, he seemed to understand that for him to attend this class, I would have to be 'along for the ride' in order to get him there and back. As young adults, when kids finally feel that a parent is looking at them in a more adult way, they actually start being somewhat 'ok' with their parents in tow. He seemed to be at that stage now.

As the weather grew a bit colder, and darkness came earlier, I would need to find a new arrangement. Luckily my son was used to me being there and appreciated my commitment. To my surprise, apparently the professor and other students had also noticed that I was facilitating my son's attendance. I guess I wasn't as 'incognito' as I thought.

I was invited and welcomed into a little office next to the classroom. It was well lighted, and comfortable. Each evening my son would head off to his classroom and I would head off to my little private office.

One evening, a bit jittery and anxious, I felt the need to take a walk around to calm my nerves. As I walked by the classroom door, I noticed that the students were engaged at computer stations and were quite intense in whatever they were doing on those computers.

My son on the other hand seemed to be floating around the class, stopping at each station to have a brief talk, do some data entry, and doing what appeared to be 'helping' a classmate to perform a task.

I was intrigued, and by the end of class exceptionally curious to find out what was going on. Instead of walking out the hallway door to our vehicle, I walked directly through the classroom to greet my son.

He, a bit unnerved I'm sure, acknowledged my presence and when I asked him what went on this evening he showed me what they were working on. It was a program called 'Train Simulator' which he had been engaged with at home for many years, and from a very young age. For his classmates it was most likely a new experience.

The professor must have noticed early on that my son needed no instruction on this particular evening. In fact, having a rather large class, he obviously decided that it would be more beneficial for my son to help his classmates maneuver through the comings and goings of the locomotives on this program.

Now my son, the youngest guy in class who was not always a talkative fellow, became the resident 'star' that evening. In this environment, he was an expert. He was very comfortable floating from station to station to assist anyone who needed his help.

As a few students continued to work after class, wanting answers to the questions they had about the program, my son continued to help them out. For those extra few minutes the professor didn't approach me, but clearly acknowledged by his facial expressions and the 'thumbs up" sign that things had gone well that evening.

Through the next few months, as the semester progressed, the cold got colder and the dark came earlier and earlier. One night, sought out by a student from my son's class, I was invited to an event. The class would be outside for an exercise in lantern symbols and protocol.

I cleared this with my son, making sure he was ok if I attended the event to 'observe'. He seemed fine with it, but I made a point to keep a distance and truly just observe.

As I watched the professor and class spread out, take the lanterns and begin the exercise, one of my son's classmates came to stand next to me. He was much older than my son, but much younger than me.

We watched together as the professor signaled the stop motion which was side to side with the lantern. After that, the signal for proceed, in an up and down arm movement. Each class member stepped up to try their skills, the opposing class group down the road yelling out what they interpreted the signal to be.

I was enjoying the demonstration and as I smiled and made brief comments to this man next to me, he seemed more interested in talking. Even though it was dark, we were under a light post, which gave me a clear view of his face.

His expression told me he had something to say, so I asked him "What do think?" expecting a comment about the lantern exercise we were observing. Instead, very polite, and very serious, choosing his words carefully, he told me that he really appreciated seeing me here supporting my son.

He proceeded to share a story about his hard-working mother who just never seemed to have the time to help him with his pursuits. She took the advice of others, that if he was to make it, he would make it on his own.

After some bumps along the road, with school, with the law, with some recreational drugs, he was finally at an age that he really could make it on his own if he wanted to. His message seemed to be that there wouldn't have been so many 'bumps' if he had had a mother like me.

I was overcome. I no longer worried that what I was doing was going to send out the wrong message to my son. Not having a drivers license, it would have taken God knows how long for him to get through this important program for his future.

This young man's words cemented my conviction to get my son through an important step in his life. He obviously had the drive, and the commitment to follow through, I was just there to facilitate.

Looking back at my own life, as my parents had 'gently' kicked me to the curb, it was the sort of thing I needed to get on with my life. I had the wherewithal, I had the smarts, and I definitely had the 'bad ass' attitude to get me into, 'or out of' any situation. If they had tried it any other way, it would have been a disaster.

That was me, this was not my son. At this time in his life, just the simple act of getting him to a venue like the museum or school had to be facilitated. He wasn't 'behind' it was that he simply needed a driver to get him where he needed to go. That driver was me.

My son would eventually finish that semester and I was able to read some great books. All was well and good, and we would move to the next step.

One night, nearing the end of the semester, pulling out of the parking lot I looked to the western sky and saw the most beautiful Harvest Moon I had ever seen. I was mesmerized by the sight and so was my son.

That huge orange moon seemed to follow us all the way home. If you are driving along on earth, moving 60 miles per hour, you feel like you are moving quite fast. If you are viewing a stellar occurrence during that drive it's as if you haven't moved at all. This moon dominated the entire night sky for our entire trip home.

Down the freeway, taking our off-ramp and now in the final stretch toward home, we both continued to watch that moon in awe. As we pulled into our court and into the driveway that Harvest Moon was absolutely, without a doubt, hanging exactly over our house.

I had not seen anything like it in my lifetime. I have not seen anything like it since.

If for no other reason, difficult as it was, I was happy that my son's need to get to school each night resulted in an experience in life I would never have had. If I had been sitting at home that evening, I would never have seen that harvest moon.

Suggestion

Supporting activities that enhance your child's life can enhance your life as well.

Chapter 12

Car Attendant

As a docent at the Railroad Museum, one was afforded many other opportunities to volunteer and serve. From the maintenance of way, which, among other things, kept the tracks repaired and clear of debris and foliage, to the car department, which worked on the upholstery and flooring to keep the cars looking good, opportunities abounded.

The shops were an opportunity to do 'hands on' work on the locomotives and cars that were in need of restoration and repair. But the big pull for my son was what he considered the best opportunity of all, becoming a car attendant on a real live train.

After a few years of being a docent, committing to every other Saturday without fail, he indicated that he was ready to move on to the dream of being a car attendant on the excursion railroad associated with the museum.

I had my doubts, but as always wanted to support any of his efforts to get "out and about" in the public arena, doing what he loved.

Once again, since he was under the age of eighteen, as part of their policy I would have to accompany him. I was not overjoyed, but of course looked into the training schedule. It would involve Saturdays and possibly some Sundays, working with the instructor and going through the protocols before we could actually be put on a crew for an excursion run.

My son and I reported the first day, not dressed appropriately because no one had bothered to tell us what "appropriate" was. Just like the first day at the museum, we seemed like fish out of water. We weren't used to being in this environment, any more than they were used to a 'pair' showing up for training, rather than an individual.

As we were 'hustled' along, with quick details along the way, it was clear to me that the crew didn't seem interested in promoting a pair to their ranks. It was obvious we did not fit their profile.

Looking back, I'm sure they felt they were "bending over backwards", to include us in the program. Talking to a few of them later, they confirmed that they had correctly assessed it wasn't good timing for either my son or me, just yet.

We struggled through the weeks of training and even though we received a nice little certificate for doing a run in a temperature in excess of 100' degrees it was a pretty miserable experience. I knew hands-down I had 'jumped the gun'. You can only imagine where I would have loved to shove that nice little certificate.

At the end of the training I told the instructor I could not support being there with my 'under-aged' son, and this would have to wait until he was eighteen and could go it alone. The relief on his face told me that he agreed.

A few years past, now eighteen and just out of high school, my son signed up, once again, for the Car Attendant class. This time I dropped him off in the morning, stayed in the air-conditioned environment of the museum as a docent, and always enjoyed those days.

He on the other hand, had to tolerate the scorching temperatures but that didn't seem to bother him a bit. I still had my doubts about whether he was ready, but he was excited and prepared to ride the rails no matter what. At the end of the day, sweaty and a bit tired out, he would have a smile you couldn't possibly wipe off his face.

At the end of the training period he would be told if he had made the cut and become part of the crew. I didn't know the process so we just kept going every other Saturday to the museum for the morning shift.

A few weeks passed and one day, as I looked out the side opening of the mail car I was assigned, I saw my son having a conversation with his Car Attendant instructor. The conversation appeared to be a solemn one. There was a lot of one-way conversation from the instructor, and a lot of head nodding from my son. I knew immediately this wasn't good, but maybe it was?

The instructor then turned and trundled along with disabilities of his own, in the direction of the mail car I was working on. He came up the back steps and clearly wanted to have a conversation with me.

He waited for the visitors to leave the exhibit. He then walked towards me with a look that told me exactly what was coming. He was choosing his words carefully, most of which included how impressed he was with my son's commitment to doing well. When asked to perform his duties, he described how polite and compliant he was. He acknowledged that my son was trying to do the best he could do.

His concern was that as long as everything went 'as planned' my son would be an asset. But, if something unusual or out of the ordinary needed attending to, he wasn't sure that my son would be a good judge of how to respond.

Compared to some of the ol' guys, who didn't speak much as they viewed the scenery of the river, only occasionally noticing that a child's head was stuck between the side-rails, my son seemed like an efficient car attendant. In reality, these same guys, should something go 'astray', would be the first up on their feet, and be ready to respond in an emergency.

I heard him out, nodded appropriately, and blew him away when I said two simple words...."I agree".

I agreed that my son was still at the point where he could go through a rote routine but be unaware of other possibilities. He was more excited about being on the train than worrying about the passengers in his charge. This train was about experience and fun but also had to have the safety of the passengers as the primary concern.

I let him know that I appreciated his input. I let him know that he was 'spot on' with his assessment. I also let him know that I appreciated the extra time and effort he had taken with this particular individual, namely my son.

We discussed the fact that given my son's nature, he would be back in the future to 'give it a go' once again. Of all the things, I think he understood this most of all, and felt better. I think he really wanted my son to succeed and was hopeful that at some point he would be a qualified car attendant.

Fortunately, a few years later, my son, more mature, would once again sign up for Car Attendant training. Unfortunately, the instructor would be someone different. But I'll always believe that his first instructor was hoping that next time my son would pass with flying colors.

He attended the training for the second time and this time he passed. He moved on to become a full-fledged member of the crew. I knew he couldn't pass unless he was in fact fully qualified so the level of my pride was 'off the charts'. I knew everyone was 'pulling for him' and that touched my heart.

Since life is full of ironies, on his very first day as a Car Attendant the unpredictable happened. Any doubts that my son could perform in a 'not so ordinary' situation was completely quelled. On his very first day as a Car Attendant the locomotive broke down part way into the mid-day run. This was a very rare occurrence, and one of the very few times the passengers would have to be evacuated and brought back to the station. Not only did he help get everyone back, it didn't seem unusually significant to him, as he was well trained to do his job.

My son and I both being much younger than most, will always be grateful for the support and effort we received from our fellow docents and train crew.

What's hard is like everyone else we continue to lose so many of those same people along the way.

It is important that if your child has a passion, something that is 'reasonable' to accomplish, you can help them through challenging times. There might also be others who can help them through challenging times if they see the passion that is there.

We are not talking about being 5' foot 3" tall and wanting a career in the NBA…that's not going to happen. What we are talking about is 'reasonable' expectations, that given their passion, you can encourage them to "try..try..and try again" if necessary. People appreciate passion and hard work when they see it. Most will go out of their way to do what they can to help.

Suggestion

Just because your child is passionate about something, doesn't guarantee success. But if people notice the passion…you may have lots of hands lifting them up.

Chapter 13

Olympics

Like me, my son has always had an interest in wildlife. Even though the majority of his vast library was filled with train related books, there was also an array of books on wildlife. He had everything from birds, to reptiles, to more exotic beasts of the jungles, not to mention the insects and spiders that 'creep me out.'

Although living in an urban area, on the outskirts, there are more rural areas that we frequented. We did enjoy a bit of wildlife along the way, but my sister and I would often joke that the most wildlife our children saw, tended to be "road kill".

Like any typical child, there were stages he did not want to do anything, even remotely related, to an activity that included me. It wasn't just out in public, but in the privacy of our own home as well. This is normal, and a sign of maturity

When he was younger we would watch TV programs together and it was always so enjoyable to be experiencing the same thing at the same time. It would lead to conversations either at the time, or at a later date, which helped us expand our communication.

If there was a program on TV about wildlife that I knew he might enjoy, rather than asking him to join me, I would simply wait until the show had started and ask him to "come take a look".

I never asked him ahead of time if he wanted to watch the program. He might refuse because he had no idea what the program would be about. And he certainly wasn't going to 'hang out' with me.

There were times when he would take a look and then venture back off into his computer room. Other times he would stand and watch for a bit, and once engaged, jump up on his chair in the family room and watch it along side me. If he engaged...great! If not, no harm, no foul.

It felt pretty good to have my "young adult son" hanging out with me once in awhile. I'm sure it helped him to be more comfortable because, not only did he have a choice in the matter he realized that sometimes my interests weren't so different from his.

As luck would have it, during one summer my son had shown an interest in watching the Olympics on TV. He was clear that it was our 'duty' to watch the Olympics each evening, making sure we followed the performances and progress of those representing our country.

I'm not sure what compelled him to commit to watching the Olympic Games, or why it was important that I participate, but I was overjoyed on both accounts. I believe engaging him periodically in watching a wildlife program together must have made him comfortable with me in the room.

He did fess-up at one point that I tended to "chatter" during a TV program, which was annoying to him, and sometimes why he didn't watch TV with me. I was working on that, and he noticed that change in me during the Olympics.

I know there are lots of guys out there who would probably give my son a "high five" for having the courage to let me know that tidbit of information. Knowing that he was just 'stating a fact', I was not insulted.

During those same Olympics a very important concept emerged. One of our top performers, a swimmer, was racking up the Gold like crazy. During the evening TV clips the camera often panned the audience for a glimpse of that Olympian's mother and her obvious pride.

My son may have realized that a mother being involved in one's adult life, this particular Olympian's life, did not make that Olympian less an individual. It was actually more of an indicator that, with the support of his mother, and seeing her pride, he might actually feel even more pride that if he had done it just for himself. It certainly didn't hurt when the camera panned down to this swimmer who was obviously waving up at his mom.

This would surface as a point of discussion for my son and me. Rather than looking at me as being overbearing at times, which I am, too opinionated at times, which I am, I could finally explain to him that as a mother I felt it was my job to support him at all cost. That was the reason I took a great interest in his activities.

I explained it like this...I imagine this Olympian's mother was likely the one who got him to each swim meet. Certainly she cheered him on from the stands as he competed. But..it was this swimmer who did all the work, who excelled on his own. She just needed to get him to the place where he could perform.

I guess with seeing a top athlete, representing our country, whose mother was actually part of the story, must have made him a little more comfortable with me hovering around.

I was simply getting him to places he needed to be in order to make sure he had opportunities. I would gladly sit in the background and wait for him to perform his duties as a docent at the museum, or a car attendant on the railroad, or drop him off to attend all his classes at college. He now seemed to understand that I was just his 'support system', but had all the faith in the world that he would perform on his own.

Either way, he was growing up and moving to that next stage. He is such a kind and thoughtful person and I knew he recognized and appreciated the daily scurrying around to get him where he needed to be, and to get myself where I needed to be as well.

He now seemed more comfortable with my presence and always thanked me at every turn. His independence would come. My letting go, would come. This was the time to finish up a lot of the things we had set out to do.

Suggestion

Don't force your older child to engage in an activity. Rather than that, ask your child to simply 'take a look'….and let your child decide.

Chapter 14

"There's No Crying in Welding"

At a relatively late stage in a long standing career, I was faced with a problem. There was what I will call, a "misunderstanding" between my manager and me. I had always been in good standing with my company so I had never considered the possibility of losing my job.

The misunderstanding was cleared up quickly, but for that brief time I realized that, should I suddenly find myself un-employed, I had no plan.

If I did, un-expectantly lose my job, keeping a roof over our heads, bills paid and food on the table was something that I was only positioned to do for a short period of time. Should the search for new employment stretch out, should securing a new job turn into a long process, I was ill-prepared.

After a bit of research into the current trends, I discovered that it was the "traditional" trades that were experiencing shortages in their work force. Shortages in areas like mechanics, machinists, welders, electricians and plumbers were resulting in a multitude of available jobs. If you had certifications, they would likely hire you if you "had a pulse."

This was a result of the baby boomers now retiring and moving out of the work force. At the same time, the younger generation moving into the work force, were more likely to pursue careers in computer technology, business and finance, marketing or education.

I had a degree and years of experience in my current career, but there was no assurance that an equivalent position would be readily available. What I needed was something that I could secure quickly, and at a good wage, while I searched for a long-term opportunity.

What fit the bill was a program at a local community college which focused on certification programs in the 'traditional' trades like machinist and welding. I decided that welding sounded pretty interesting and in a few short months I could complete a program that would qualify me for several local jobs at a good wage. It was a night school program so I could continue my current job, as long as they would have me.

As a matter of coincidence....one of the most revered skills in the railroad industry is welding. If you knew nothing else, could care less about engines or cars, the railroad industry was always in need of certified welders. After the summer when my son and I had been reacquainted with spending time together by watching the Olympics, I felt comfortable asking him to consider taking a welding class with me. This could help him get on with a railroad.

As I shared information and did a bit of coaxing, I somehow convinced my son to take this welding class. Mind you, it was my goal to acquire the skills of welding, but once I pulled up the myriad of job postings for welders at Union Pacific a BNSF he seemed more amenable to the idea. The job postings for welders at railroad companies all across the country seemed endless.

I promised that I would go in one door, and he could enter the class through another door. No one would be the wiser and he would not have to go through the degradation of having his mom 'tag along'. Luckily he was just now getting to the age where I was less of an embarrassment and more of just an accepted 'pain in the ass.'

We were signed up for welding class, and looking back, thankfully, had no idea what we were getting into. Like railroad operations at the community college level, the welding classes were at night, catering to a population that already had day jobs and were looking for new opportunities for a real career.

It was standing-room only on the first day of class. Clearly, this was a course that interested many individuals who had likely done the same kind of research I had done. These were individuals who were serious about learning a skill that could pay off in terms of permanent employment, regardless of the economic times.

This was not your typical collegiate classroom. It was not made up of young kids who were attending classes until they decided on what they were going to do with the rest of their lives. It was not a class that represented the diversity in our social make-up. It in no, way, shape, or form even remotely resembled a group that would welcome someone like me or my son to the club.

This was a somewhat 'scruffy' group. There was only one other female besides me and she was much younger. She was a cowgirl type, drove a pick-up, and I suspect carried some kind of fire-arm underneath the seat of that pick-up.

The guys on average were within the age range of my son. However, their tattoos clearly represented a life-style quite different from his. Some seemed genuinely interested in pursuing a welding career, while others looked as if they were here because of one last ultimatum from their probation officer.

The instructor entered the room in his baseball cap, work shirt, jeans and boots. He was a hard read in terms of attitude, but clearly, was not a "high-five" kind of guy. His sole purpose for this first class session became clear. He had to make sure there would only be enough students left by the second session to allow each student to have a booth in the welding lab.

He commenced to explain why we were all here that day. We all wanted to learn welding, but he had to set us straight on what that meant. He proceeded to share stories about real life experiences in his career, adding in various scenarios of what could happen right here in the classroom.

With a very calm and cool demeanor, he outlined these possible scenarios. We would be working with very high levels of electrical power that, if used improperly, could blow us across the room. If we were lucky we would recover from the blow, if unlucky, it would cause a heart arrhythmia and he would have to call paramedics who would hopefully arrive quickly. Although he was certified in CPR, he mentioned that he was not very fond of actually performing the task.

He described the gases and flames that, if not handled correctly, would set us on fire. If we didn't "stop, drop and roll" the result would likely be serious bodily harm.

He cautioned about our ability to "listen". He shared a story about a student who had apparently 'not' listened when he made it clear, and emphasized, that you should never put a finger into the drop slot on the metal cutter.

He described an occasion when he heard lots of commotion and went to the source. What he found were several students gathered around the metal cutter, searching for something that appeared to be "lost".

Deducing that the ashen-faced student with a pool of blood underneath him was now likely missing a finger, he approached what was now the fingerless one. He asked this student to sit down. The student shared with him that he was in a lot of pain....his response..."yeah, I imagine you are."

He made a call to 911. The class found the missing appendage and sent it along in the ambulance. He made sure the student had his tuition reimbursed.

You could have heard a "pin drop" in the classroom after that story. I can't imagine what my son was thinking at that point, and did not have the heart to look behind me, to where he was sitting.

The second session came, and although the class size had been cut in half, there was still some weeding out to do. This session was focused on the requirements for equipment and supplies.

The instructor seemed quite comfortable that after a thorough review of those requirements, the last few folks would drop the class. This would mean by session three we would be down to the core number he had in mind to conduct a meaningful program.

He, of course, was right. We reviewed the metal requirements that had to be cut and purchased at a local supplier. We reviewed the flame-retardant jackets and pants, not to mention boots that could not have shoe strings due to fire potential.

There were tools, grinders and safety goggles as well. There were tips and bits and gloves that had to be to the correct specifications. All in all it was a huge investment, and for a starving college student, not likely something they were prepared for. They were offered "leftovers" from previous classes but he made it clear that the helmets were not necessarily "lice free"…and the jackets and pants hadn't been out for cleaning since his arrival which was several years before.

Session three, all was right with the world. We were down to a reasonable class size, my son and I still attending. He already seemed surprised at that fact.

As we proceeded though the first few weeks of lectures, textbook homework and safety tests all seemed comfortable. In the following weeks we would don our gear and get into the lab. That's when things got 'crazy'.

On the first day out into the lab I talked to other class members and discovered that they had some experience. With the exception of two other students, we were the only ones who had not taken a previous course with Professor R.

Although we didn't sit together, or converse much, the instructor seemed interested in our relationship. He had an office well away from the main entrance but I imagine, on occasion, through the classroom windows he would see us arrive together.

It didn't take much for him to put "two and two together". As we ventured out into the lab for a demonstration, and then a first try at using our equipment to actually weld something, he made sure to call up all the other students except us. There we were...the last two, waiting to get that first 'hands-on' experience with welding.

As he called my son to the table, giving him the instructions he needed to get started, he looked back a few times, clearly wanting to get my reaction to this particular's student's performance. He appeared to be surprised, when my son had no trepidation, listened well, and fired up his gun as requested.

As the sparks flew, and the professor figured out my son was a 'lefty'...the direction was adjusted and my son performed his first welding task to a level that determined he could be sent off to his assigned booth.

Now it was just Professor R and me. I approached the table for my instructions. He put everything in place and ordered me to proceed. It was a disaster.

First, I had forgotten to put on my reading glasses underneath the safety goggles, so I could barely see the placement of my gun onto the crease in the metal I was suppose to weld together. Second, I had purchased the 'top of the line' helmets, which I found out later blacked out if any sunlight was in close proximity. The table of course was just inside an open door with sunlight streaming in. I was essentially working 'in the dark'.

The professor 'not so kindly' decided to help by standing behind me to help me guide the welding gun. He did not 'gently' guide my arm, he grabbed my arm sternly. He assisted me in moving the gun across the appropriate area until he was frustrated enough to call it quits.

Clearly agitated…he turned and asked me, "How do you know him?" referring to my son of course, I responded…"I know him".

Taking it to a higher decibel, he asked "HOW do you know him?"…I responded at an equally higher decibel, "I KNOW him".

Now, almost at a level of a scream, he makes a statement more than asks a question and says…"HE'S YOUR KID!?".

I looked him in the eye, did not respond, and that was all the answer he needed.

Even though my son and I were under no obligation to share our personal information, it did somehow seem wrong. I don't think Professor R understood, any more than I understood, why we were both frustrated with the situation. We just were.

There was some sort of holiday and a long weekend so we would not be back in class for several days. That encounter just sort of sat there in my mind, and ate away at me.

I pulled my thoughts together and decided to confront the situation with what is always the best course of action…"straight on".

We arrived early on that following Monday, unloaded our gear and I sought out Professor R, who was in his office with his lab assistant. I did not ask his permission to speak, I just proceeded.

I described a scenario to him, in the form of a question. What if a father and son walked into your classroom a few weeks back and boldly acknowledged that they were here to take your class 'together'…to learn welding 'together'?

I continued to talk, telling him that I imagine there would have been a lot of 'ball grabbing' and 'high-fives'…"Right?" There would have been ample amounts of good will, and no one would consider that a dad and his son taking this course together would be a problem…"Right?"

I continued on my soapbox and explained to him that 'dad' was in North Carolina and my son was 'stuck with me'. Further, if he had any issues, I knew he was within his rights to drop us. He could use safety issues or 'high maintenance' issues, or disruption issues, but I acknowledged that he had the power to drop us from the class.

Last of all I told him, "You can drop us, you can fail us, but we will NOT quit."

Neither his dad nor I ever taught our son that quitting was an option just because things get tough. It is OK to fail, it is OK to try again, but it is NOT OK to quit, and live wondering whether or not you would have made it.

In a perfect world, one would think my views were considered and things would get easier. It is not a perfect world. If anything, things got tougher. We now had to prove ourselves and we had to stay up with the group. There would be no latitude.

I did notice that the lab assistant spent extra time with us and Professor R acknowledged that we needed this assistance, as we had not taken previous courses like the rest of the class.

We continued to attend every class and get perfect scores on homework and tests. When we were in the lab I was afforded assistance to turn on the gas and equipment that was placed at a level I could not reach due to my height, or lack thereof.

I always considered myself a fairly good and dedicated parent. As I walked by my son's welding booth one session, sparks flying, molten metal dripping from the piece of metal as he performed an overhead welding assignment, I seriously questioned what I had gotten him into. I thought to myself…"I must be out of my mind".

Each day when we packed up to go to class I had a pit in my stomach, and felt like crying. There was nothing said on the first day of class, nothing in the text book, and no mention in the syllabus of any rule, but you just had a gut level feeling that there is "no crying in welding".

The weeks slid by and in the last week it was time to present our projects and clean up the lab. It was Christmas season and we all brought some goodies to the last class. I presented Professor R with a Santa hat full of things he mentioned he liked.

I expected a 'growl' and a look of distain. Instead, he removed the booty from the hat and proceeded to put it on his head. He actually smiled, and I had to remind myself again that there was no crying in welding. I think Professor R and I both learned a lot in those weeks.

That was the best day. Professor R ran around in his Santa hat, barking orders at all of us. We all pitched in to clean up the lab and according to the syllabus, our participation that day was a big part of our grade.

We were done. Grades didn't matter...we finished! The relief was second only to the pride that my son and I had. We had taken on a very hard task together and I gained a renewed knowledge of where my son was in dealing with the 'bigger world'. My son may well have gained the knowledge that, still a "pain in the ass"...I wasn't so bad after all.

It was important for me to be on an even playing field with my son, at this older age. By taking this course together I had first-hand knowledge of what was going on, and had an opportunity to discuss things with him, knowing the details behind the scenes.

I had an opportunity to really see his character, really see what he was capable of, and understand that other people could see that too.

Sometime later, as my son signed up for classes for the next semester, he had to run his transcripts. It was on that day he discovered he actually received an "A" in welding.

I never ran my transcripts, I don't know what my grade was, but whatever it is, it isn't important.

Suggestion

If you decide to engage in an event, or activity, or take a class with your young adult child, make sure it is NOT welding.

Chapter 15

Pulling Out of the Station

When boarding a train, one must take along all the things needed for the upcoming trip. When pulling out of the station one hopes one has packed every necessary provision to get them down the track to whatever destination they are meant to get to.

When the time comes, I know that I'll be helping my son to pack clothes, pajamas, socks and clean underwear for his trip down the track, into his life. He'll be fine...I'll be a mess. He will pull out of the station and travel down the tracks he is destined to travel.

It won't be the pants or shirts or the right jacket in that baggage that's important. It will be the baggage he carries containing all the things I tried to teach him, and all the things he learned about himself, that will be important.

Getting him through high school and on to college, supporting him as a Museum Docent and Car Attendant meant the world to me. More important, it was a time when he began to realize that, given all the challenges he had to face, he had accomplished something very big. He realized that in spite of me, he could take responsibility for those accomplishments in his own right.

It was no longer as important that I was proud of him, but that he took pride in himself.

When he graduated from high school, and had a plan in place to attend a local community college, a very good neighbor, who had taken a special interest in him, wanted to give him a gift. She drove to the school, purchased a few
T-shirts with the college's logo and gave them as a gift to him a few weeks before he started to college.

When she presented him with the T-shirts it was a confirmation, this was now "real". He would have a new school. He was now moving on to the next level in life. He would finally feel this sense of 'personal' accomplishment, personal "pride" that no matter what someone else tells you, it doesn't mean as much, as when you feel it for yourself 'inside'.

Over the next few years as he attended college, those T-shirts were a regular part of his attire. Whether it was at school, or a family event, or just down to the local market, he wore them with pride, acknowledging "if asked" that yes, he was a student at this college.

After the T-shirts had been worn and washed, what seemed like hundreds of times, they were finally retired to his "at home" wardrobe, along with sweat pants, when he was just hanging out at home.

Eventually you could practically read through these T-shirts from all the wear and tear but you'll never believe this...he still didn't get rid of them for years to come, as he didn't have the heart to let them go. The pride he had when he put on those T-shirts reflected the pride he carried in his heart.

Somewhere in this time frame, as he was attending college, being a Docent at the Museum and a Car Attendant on a railroad, and more, my son and I had developed a 'ritual'. I periodically on a very good day, or on just the right occasion, would share a thought with him. I would say "I'm proud of you".

He would, and still does, respond in a way that makes me know that what I sought out to do, was in fact accomplished. When I tell him "I'm proud of you", his response is immediate, and sincere..."And I'm proud of myself!"

Acknowledgments

Thanks to my "J" Team....Joe, Janet, Janey, Jan, and Gerry ('G' pronounced as a "J" anyway).

To Joe ...thanks for bringing accuracy to each chapter. Making the story what it was meant to be, in the order in which it was meant to be told.

To Janet...thanks for your time and for your candor. Your expertise made me appear to be a much better writer than I am.

To Janey...thanks for your work, contributing to each chapter with sentences and verbiage that made more sense. Conveying more accurately what I was trying to say.

To Jan... without your beautiful artwork the books would never be what they are. With your 'heartfelt' illustrations, you brought each chapter to life!

To Gerry...who took whatever material I brought, in whatever condition I brought it, and made it into 'real live' books.

To my mom...who when I jumped off that cliff into a new life, was the parachute that made me feel I would land softly. I'm sure we dragged Dad along "kicking and screaming" but I know in the end he landed softly too.

To my sister and to my Aunt Barbara...your words expressing your pride in me, inspired me to keep going. You made me feel like a little girl, a little girl who found strength from the women around her.

To my Boise family...who appreciated what I was doing. Especially to one particular young lady who gave me the ultimate compliment when she began reading the first book on Christmas day, the day she received it, and stayed up until the 'the wee hours of the morning' to finish it.

To my Montana family...your inspiring words, your feedback and enthusiasm, brought me peace. It made me realize that what I was doing was the right thing.

And finally, to my son...using your passion for trains allowed me to teach you things you needed to know. Having you in my life and loving you the way I do, taught me things I needed to know.

Printed by Libri Plureos GmbH in Hamburg, Germany